A TIME TO DIE

Glenn M. Vernon

 University Press of America

The Authors:
Glenn M. Vernon is Professor of Sociology, University of Utah

Robert W. Gardner is Assistant Professor of Sociology, Walla Walla
    College, Walla Walla, Washington

Michael R. Leming is Assistant Professor of Sociology, St. Olaf
    College, Northfield, Minnesota

William D. Payne is Ass't. Director, Utah State Division of
    Alcoholism and Drugs, Salt Lake City, Utah

J. D. Robson is Assistant Professor of Sociology, University of
    Arkansas at Little Rock

Charles E. Waddell is Assistant Professor of Sociology, University
    of Western Australia, Nedlands, Western Australia

The following are reprinted with permission
Glenn M. Vernon and William D. Payne. Myth-Conceptions about Death.
    Journal of Religion and Health, vol.12 no.1 January 1973
    pp. 63-76

Glenn M. Vernon. Dying as a Social-Symbolic Process. Humanitas,
    vol. X, No. 1, February 1974, pp. 21-32

Glenn M. Vernon and Charles E. Waddell. Dying as Social Behavior:
    Mormon Behavior Through Half a Century. Omega, vol. 5, no. 3
    1974, pp. 199-206

Glenn M. Vernon. Death Control. Omega, vol. 3, May 1972, pp. 131-138.

The following has been accepted for publication
Glenn M. Vernon. Disguised Theologians: The Anti-immortalists. Omega.

The following have been submitted for publication
Glenn M. Vernon. "...And a Time to Die."

Glenn M. Vernon. Myth-Conceptions Concerning Death Related Behavior.

TABLE OF CONTENTS

CHAPTER 1

". . . AND A TIME TO DIE"

Glenn M. Vernon

Bible readers are told that "To everything there is a season... A time to be born and a time to die." Our contemporary age has developed into a time to think seriously and at times publicly about death, and to analyze death-related behavior. It would, accordingly, seem to be appropriate to consider, as we will in this article, just what "a time to die" means.

Analysis here will focus more upon timing than upon dying, emphasizing that there are different types of time systems and that time phenomenon is more complex than is frequently assumed. Most of us function effectively within different time systems at different times. We usually move with ease from one to the other. We don't identify these different systems very often, however. The difference between the two time systems with which we are concerned is contained in the following questions:

Does a person die when his time is up

OR

Is a person's time up when he dies?

To which type of time does the Biblical statement refer?

One type of time is clock time. This is the time with which most people are most familiar and which they experience most often. Scientists frequently use clock time in their experiments. Bureaucratic behavior is clock-timed interaction. One of the first things a growing child is taught is to tell time--clock time. It is easy to assume that this basic (some would say "only") time is the time to which the Biblical statement refers.

The statement that a person dies when his time is up involves mechanical clock-time. The statement incorporates a scripted, pre-programmed aspect, suggesting that when the clock, or the calendar "reads" or reaches a given time, a person is scheduled to die. The time runs out and his biology runs out simultaneously. The two are somehow locked together. Such a time system is involved in the story of the person who fearfully fled his home to escape the death which he believed to be there for him, only to find that death was waiting for him to attive at his new destination.

In such an interpretation, events conspire or some directing force arranges that the person will die on schedule--on time. We live in an orderly world, and we die in an orderly manner--all according to time, pre-determined, scripted clock time.

The belief that a person dies when his time is up is by some related to the belief that God calls a person home, or that the time of one's dying is determined by God. God decides when a given person will die. Such an interpretation is frequently used in interpretations of the dying time of the young and the prominent. Such deaths are typically difficult to accept and those who introduce the "time was up" interpretation apparently see this as an interpretation which makes the actual death more easily acceptable. The statement from Ecclesiastes used to introduce this article may be used to support such an interpretation.

The statement incorporates a human responsibility-evading component. If a person dies according to God's schedule, God is responsible, not us. We should accept what God does and not doubt or question His wisdom. We die at the convenience of God and accept such a death without questioning it. We thus remove some of the "sting" from death.

An alternate interpretation, reflected in the statement that a person's time is up when he dies, is that time is an event-time system, or a "time as a capsule" system. Clock time is a rigid, predetermined system in which each element or unit is of the same predetermined length and one follows the other in predetermined and hence predictable fashion. One minute, one day, one year is of the same identical length everywhere, and any time. In an event-time system, the units or component parts are flexible, socially constructed, ever-changing phenomenon. Growing time to the Indian is what happens between the planting of the seed corn and the ripening of the ears. Growing time is not rigidly predetermined but rather is influenced by a whole series of internal and external factors, and varies from season to season. There is always a growing time, but each growing time is, in effect, "it's own person." Each is its own event.

The event of living or a person's living time or growing time is up when he dies. In this statement, the actual dying is not pre-programmed in any rigid sense. That one will die is pre-programmed. Everyone has a time to die. This time will eventually arrive, but no one "knows the hour." A person's actual living time and hence dying time is, as with the corn, influenced by a complex set of interrelated internal and external factors, and it varies from season to season and from person to person. If there are any determining factors (using "determining" in a strong sense) they are not pre-programmed, scripted or blueprinted. Each person's living time is spent influencing his time of dying. Everything a person does and many things which happen in his society and in his environment directly or indirectly influence the event.

A person's time is up when he dies. Dying marks the end of an event. Knowing the time of birth and the time of death permits the living to establish symboled boundary lines around an event and treat it or consider it as an entity. When a person dies his time is up. A boundary has been established.

Viewing dying as an event-time phenomenon, shifts the focus to humans, and thus incorporates a human-responsibility component. If an event is influenced by social and environmental factors, it is the social-environmental factors which are responsible for the event, not supernatural factors. The dying time is influenced by an entire lifetime of experiences and decisions,

2

including decisions about occupation, life style, eating, diet, driving, associating, loving, vacationing, working, etc. The causes of a given non-accidental death are much more extensive than just what happens immediately prior to that death. They are woven into the living fabric of the life-time event. Even an accidental death has many factors which in effect make the "accident happen."

"To everything there is a season..." The "season" concept suggests an event-time system rather than a clock-time system. Physical, natural seasons, for instance, never coincide exactly with calendar-time seasons. What constitutes spring is never the same from season to season. "Spring-ing" or " autumn-ing" is an event of nature, which is constructed as it progresses. It is not the pre-scripted, scheduled event that the calendar suggests. Spring's time is up when it dies. Spring doesn't die when its time is up.

Neither do people.

CHAPTER 2

MYTH-CONCEPTIONS ABOUT DEATH

Glenn M. Vernon
William D. Payne

This paper concerns the meaning of death. Meaning is social-symbolic phenomenon provided by man. It does not reside in that to which meaning is given. Meaning is socially constructed. The meaning of anything, then, is always potentially challengeable and changeable. Distortions or myth-conceptions of one type or another may be incorporated in the accepted meaning of anything. The meaning of death is no exception.

In the United States, death is a topic surrounded by a symbolic taboo screen that colors the way in which it is perceived and, in fact, discourages looking directly at the phenomenon. Questions likely to identify myth-conceptions then, are frequently not even asked. Any characteristic such as a taboo screen that contributes to ambiguity of perception facilitates the development of a variety of interpretations of what is perceived and a variety of experiences with that phenomenon. The taboo characteristic of the experiences of Americans with death has facilitated the development of certain myths, which it is the purpose of this paper to discuss. The origins of the myths are not known, although hypotheses about them have been developed in some cases.

Efforts have been made especially in the last ten years or so to remove some of the taboo or negative definitions of death. Various social scientists have begun to use their skills in an effort to provide more scientific understanding of death. In the process it has been discovered that some of the widely accepted beliefs about death do not seem to be substantiated by the evidence available or by the perceptual-analytical tools being used. This illustrates a basic point of the sociology of knowledge that the answers one gets to his questions are always relative to the method used to secure them.

Attention will be given here to what appear to be some of the major myths or myth-conceptions about death. These myths are not necessarily endorsed by everyone, but certainly enjoy widespread acceptance.

4

Man's interpretations of man's behavior in general have followed a broad trend. Early supernatural determinism was replaced by biological-individualistic determinism, which, in turn, is being replaced by social-symbolic determinism. In supernatural deterministic interpretations, supernatural beings or forces were seen as major causative factors in human behavior. In biological determinism interpretations, biological factors were in effect deified and seen as major causative factors in human behavior. A social-symbolic interpretation views biological factors as influencing but not determining human interaction. Biological factors are necessary but not sufficient factors. Behavior is seen as a socially and symbolically created phenomenon. Such an interpretation is presented here.

Since the social scientist restricts attention to what is empirical, he of necessity ignores the question of whether supernatural forces of one kind or another are involved. Many of the myth-conceptions relative to death incorporate aspects of biological determinism. Death is accordingly viewed as essentially a biological phenomenon. Such a perspective tends to ignore the social-symbolic dimensions thereof.

There is a scapegoating potential of biological determinism and supernatural determinism. Man may attribute to these sources consequences for which in fact he is responsible. If God is seen as causing death, or if biology is seen as the cause of death, one is not likely even to consider the social-symbolic causes of death. In part, this paper questions the value of preserving the belief that biological factors are the major cause of death or that biological survival is somehow inherently the most important aspect of life. Most of the myth-conceptions we shall analyze are rooted in the basic premise that biology should ipso facto be given greater importance than other factors, or that biological factors will determine behavior regardless of how defined.

If one starts his analysis from the basic premises of biological determinism or supernaturalism, he ends up with an interpretation of behavior that sees biological or supernatural factors as causing behavior. The human ability to define a situation in a certain way and then to act on the basis of those definitions regardless of their accuracy is often ignored in discussions of death. The involvement of human beings in that behavior then can be disregarded. The responsibility of human beings for their own behavior can be disregarded. The classical scapegoating process can be undertaken, in which the responsibility is placed upon man's biology and upon the supernatural.

Six myth-conceptions about death will now be reviewed and analyzed.

5

I. Myth conception: An individual cannot conceive of his own death.

Many philosophers have made the observation with Oraison that " . . . I cannot experience my cessation, and I cannot even conceive of it or imagine it. The only experience I can have is the cessation of another person." (Oraison, 1969) Freud likewise maintained an individual could conceive of the death of others but not himself. (Freud, 1918) We always survive ourselves as spectators in any attempt of this nature, or we never get away from the fact that it is a living being who is doing the conceiving. Sumner and Keller, early American sociologists, suggested the same inability as indicating that man is helpless when he tries to conceive of a state of nonexistence. (Sumner and Keller, 1927)

When an individual conceives of his own death he must be both subject and object, definer and the defined, the knower and the known. How, then, argue some, can a being with an awareness conceive of himself without that awareness when the awareness is needed for the process of conceiving? The notion "I am dead" is a paradox, according to Weisman and Hackett. (Weisman and Hackett, 1961:323-356)

However, an understanding of the symbolic nature of human behavior and of self-definitions involved in behavior does not necessarily lead to the conclusion that man cannot conceive of his own demise. The capacity to define and redefine is almost limitless in human beings. In a sense, man conceives of anything for which he creates symbols.

All people apply definitions to themselves. Thus it is not uncommon for an individual to be both the definer and the defined. Neither is it uncommon for a person to conceive of himself or other aspects of his social world inaccurately. Alfred Stern reminds us that "sense experience is not the bridge which connects us with, but the abyss which separates us from absolute reality." (Stern, 1956: 291) Man is never able to know (in some absolute, nonsymbolic sense) the "referent world." Symbols represent but do not duplicate the referent or the phenomenon to which they refer. Man's symbolizing behavior is more an artist's conception of the world than a photographic duplication of it. A conception of being dead is not being dead. It is a symbolic construction of being dead.

While it is true that conception of anything, present or future, real or imagined, is always to some degree inaccurate, there would seem to be no valid reason for doubting whether an individual can conceive of his own death as accurately as he can conceive of the death of others or any future or imagined condition. Accuracy of conceptions is not as important in understanding human behavior as is the fact that human beings do create definitions about death and dying, even of their own death.

6

II. Myth conception: The meaning of life is death.

Since death appears to be the end of every living being, many have concluded with Jung that "The meaning of life is death." (Jung, 1959:3-15) Bromberg and Schilder suggest that all libidinous instincts find an extensive expression
in the idea of death. (Bromberg and Schilder, 1933:133-185) All libidinous roads
lead to death and thus, they suggest, death becomes the perfect symbol of life.
Hartland refers to death as a "cardinal condition of existence." (Hartland, 1928:
411-444) In his discussion of beliefs about the origin of death he suggests that
they "all exhibit the universal incredibility of mankind as to the naturalness and
necessity of death." Malinowski, in addition, identities death as the supreme
and final crisis of life. (Malinowski, 1926)

While there is no reason to doubt that biological death is a consequence
of all biological life and that all living things are moving toward death, it does
not follow that life exists just for the purpose of death and that what happens between birth and death is devoid of human meaning. Such statements as those
above lead to at least three misleading conclusions. First, that there is one or
more major meanings to life. Such an interpretation ignores the multidimension-
ality of meanings attached to everything, including death and life. Death, for
example, is biological, and the biological aspects are given meanings; but it also
has many social aspects that are given meaning. Man labels death phenomena,
and he responds to the labels or symbolic meanings, not to the biological facts
per se. Meanings attached to dying are only a few of the meanings a person experiences in life. Meanings attached to death itself are only a part of the meanings attached to dying. In fact, if titles of articles in books and journals on death
are any indication, studies of death seem to look at everything but the actual biological death of a being.

Second, such statements would lead one to believe that biological death is
the supreme and final meaning in life. Vrijhof questions this conclusion. (Vrijhof, 1967:29-60) He asks, "Why after all, must death and suffering be regarded
as the ultimate problem of human life?" and Carlozzi asks if death really is the
final act in which a person can "participate." (Carlozzi, 1970:27) He argues
that the advent of organ transplants gives some new meaning to the "finality of
death."

Finally, such statements lead one to believe that since death is inevitable,
each death is also "natural." Some deaths, however, are more "natural" than
others. The term "natural death" connotes biological malfunctioning in old age,
which man is unable to prevent medically. Such a concept masks the deaths due
to famine, accident, illness, war, suicide, pollution, and a host of other "causes"
that, to a great extent, are social in origin. When man is capable of intervening
in the course of nature, our definition of what is "natural" undergoes modification.

7

III. Myth conception: Death or being dead is a clearly identifiable condition.

To dichotomize the living and the dead into two completely separate categories divided by the moment of death is to ignore the continuity of life and death. It might be useful for several reasons to think in terms of a continuum of death, or at least to recognize that there are several ways in which a person might be defined as "dead." Fred Rosner feels differences in a definition of death are common and even among the medical community there is no unanimity of opinion or uniformity of criteria. He says: "Until recently, cessation of respiration and absence of discernible heart beat or pulse sufficed for the physician to pronounce an individual dead. In this age of electroencephalograms, electrocardiograms, pacemakers, respirators, defibrillators and other sophisticated diagnostic and therapeutic machinery, the classic definition of death is being reevaluated." (Rosner, 1969:105)

Hartland indicates that some groups practice burial of individuals whom Americans would consider to be alive. The Abipones, fearing that the sight of death or the dying would reduce the warrior's willingness to do battle, got rid of the dead and dying with great speed, defining them all as "dead." (Hartland, 1928:411-444)

Two misconceptions concerning death definitions identified by Schneidman are 1) the belief that the concept of "death" is operationally sound, and 2) the belife that the traditional classifications of death phenomena are clear. (Schneidman, 1963:201-227)

There is a meaningful distinction between the biological fact or process of death and the social awareness and symbolization of death (biological death and symbolic death). Kalish subdivides biological death into biological and clinical death. (Kalish, 1966:3) Biological death occurs when the organs cease to function; clinical death when the organism ceases to function. Joseph Still identifies five levels of death and suggests the complexity not only of the question of when death occurs, but also the question of when life begins. (Still, 1970:66-74) A committee of the Harvard Medical School suggests that irreversible coma be used as a criterion for death, one reason being that present technology permits a body to be kept functioning even though the brain is extensively and irreversibly damaged. (Beecher et al., 1968:337)

Even less agreed upon than the physiological aspects of death are the social and symbolic aspects. Symbolic death may also be subdivided into cases where an individual defines himself as dead or "as good as dead" and cases where

8

others define the patient as hopeless. The latter situation is depicted by the nurse who, after hearing that her mother had been diagnosed as having terminal cancer, said, "My mother died for me at the moment I heard the diagnosis--I didn't even shed a tear when she finally expired." Weisman and Hackett make the same point in distinguishing between two kinds of denial--denial by the patient and denial of the patient. (Weisman and Hackett, 1967:79-110)

For many, symbolic death precedes biological death. Knight and Herter report the readjustments a family was forced to make when the father, because of the severity of his condition, was defined as dead by his family. His surprising recovery forced construction of new ties for those broken in an "anticipatory grief" process. (Knight and Herter, 1969:196-201)

To many persons, the realization of the death of a loved one may not occur at the time of biological death. The meaning of death comes gradually. Kastenbaum suggests that a social death occurs in the elderly in that they are treated as "half-dead" even though they are still physically alive. (Kastenbaum, 1969: 28-54) Still others accept religious definitions of death as a temporary separation of loved ones. Death may have quite different meanings for different people.

IV. Myth conception: There is a biologically given instinct for biological self-preservation.

There is a widely-accepted belief that man instinctively strives to preserve himself biologically. Stringfellow, writing in 1963, for example, indicated that death is adverse to the most profound and elementary self-interest of a person or society--the mere preservation of life. He further suggests that the fear of death, especially one's own, is the most universal dread men suffer. (Stringfellow, 1963)

Mayer gives the following interpretation of the instinct for self-preservation:

Proof enough of the life instinct, if (as Goethe and Luther insist) the bargain is a bad one and still we cling to it. Did not Satan say of Job, "All that a man hath will he give for his life," and the Lord reply "save his life?" Did not the first psychologist and every psychologist since, say that self-preservation is the first law of nature? But then life is good, no matter how bad, and better than death however good. (Mayer, 1965:107-164)

Interpretations that account for self-preservation behavior on the basis of a biological instinct overlook the distinctive manner in which symbols, especially value definitions, are involved in human behavior. Anything, including life, can

9

be defined in any number of different ways. Men can define life as undesirable and death as desirable, and those definitions will be very salient for their behavior. Dorothy Lee writes that she can find no record of a society in which the preservation of life is valued above all else. For everyone, she suggests, there is some cause for which he will give his life. (Lee, 1959:72)

Research involving prisoners of war arrives at a similar conclusion. For everyone there are certain types of living or certain experiences that are defined as worse than death. (Rosenberg, Gerver, and Howton, 1964:159; Mayer, 1965: 107-164)

The behavior of an individual occurs in response to symbols and is relative to the audience and the specific situation. Soldiers face death without retreating. Pickpockets were found plying their trade at public hangings of pickpockets in England. Martyrs have rejoiced in becoming martyrs for their faith. Individuals have given their lives to protect others. Many take their own lives when they define death as preferable to life. Hinton extracts the following from the letter of a Kamikaze pilot, "Please congratulate me. I have been given the splendid opportunity to die. This is my last day. The destiny of our homeland hinges on the decisive battle . . . where I shall fall like a blossom from a radiant cherry tree." (Hinton, 1967:47, 95)

Cappon suggests that, if we accept a person's verbal responses, life is not one's most valuable possession. (Cappon, 1959:466-489) In fact, in his research, willingness to give one's life was associated with physical and emotional adjustment. In his study, only 36 percent of those in a mental hospital indicated that they would offer their lives under any circumstance for anything or anybody. Eighty-one percent of his normative sample indicated conditions under which they would give their lives. Cappon concludes that in North America today one's family and not one's life is the dearest possession--not only the actual family, but also the idea of family, because responses did not vary significantly when the person was unwed, childless, or parentless.

Sorenson summarized American values in life, concluding that to Americans life is precious--the more of it, both quantitatively and qualitatively, that can be preserved the better. However, death has greater value in special circumstances. (Sorenson, 1956)

V. Myth conception: A dying person should not be told he is dying.

Informing the terminally ill person of his condition is not a popular task. Kalish indicates that such confrontations in hospitals are frequently avoided by ward personnel at all costs. (Kalish, 1965:87-96) In avoiding the subject, they are at times "obviously and ridiculously optimistic" in their patient contacts. Feifel reports from his research that some of the professional personnel with whom he had contact indicated that, as a matter of policy, they never told a patient that he had a serious illness from which he could die. "The one thing you never do," they emphasized, "is to discuss death with a patient." (Feifel, 1963:12, also 11, 17)

In research that has studied the beliefs of physicians on this point, between 69 and 90 percent of the doctors, depending on the study, were in favor of not telling the patient that he was dying. (Kasper, 1959:259-270, also 17) In his sample of 80 bereaved Britishers, Gorer found without exception that, even though relatives might have been informed by the doctor or hospital, the dying man or woman was kept in ignorance. (Gorer, 1967:2) He then goes on to question the ethics of this medical practice. Frequently-given reasons for maintaining a terminal patient in ignorance of his condition are: Seriously ill patients are afraid to think about death; therefore, one should not add to their problems (Feifel, 1963:12, also 11, 17); terminal patients really don't wish to know they are dying (Glaser, 1965:30-31); or patients might give way to despair and possible suicide. (Gorer, 1967:2)

The reactions of a majority of patients and potential patients to the possibility of being kept ignorant of the fact that they were dying is contrary to these beliefs. Kasper indicates that from 77 to 89 percent say they would want to know if they were dying. (Kasper, 1959:259-270, also 17) Of the 60 patients studied by Feifel 82 percent reported that they would prefer to be informed about their condition. (Feifel, 1963:12, also 11, 17) In a subsequent study of physicians it was found that an overwhelming majority of these physicians wanted to be informed if they had an incurable disease; but they were less willing than the patients involved in the study to provide such information to others in the same situation. (Feifel, et al., 1967:201-202) When asked, "If you contracted a fatal illness do you feel that you would want to be told that you would most likely die?" Vernon in a nonpatient sample found 71 percent said "yes" while only 15 percent said "no." (Vernon, 1970:121)

Even when a doctor carefully avoids any mention of the possibility of death, his attitude and that of others often subtly conveys to the patient his terminal condition. Hinton indicates that "Only a few people now assert that no one ever realizes that they are dying." (Hinton, 1967:47, also 93) He quotes a doctor with

11

wide experience with hospital deaths as saying, "In my own experience I find that the truth dawns gradually on many, even most, of the dying even when they do not ask and are not told." "The question is hardly ever, should he be told?, but rather, how shall we deal with what we must assume he knows? It is a problem not of fact but of relationship." (Reeves, 1969:5-9)

Others have found that patients who had not been told of their fatal illness did, in fact, know they were dying and were relieved to be able to discuss that fact freely with their doctor. (Shield, 1966:17)

When we refuse to recognize that a person is dying, or let him know that we are aware of his dying behavior, we impose an isolation upon him. Such agreed upon silence may increase the patient's fears and despair while at the same time cutting him off from the opportunity to reduce those anxieties through sympathetic discussion or some type of therapy. Some patients suffer more from the emotional isolation and unwitting rejection than from an illness per se. Feifel suggests that an individual who is dying may feel less isolated when he is able to share his feelings and thoughts about dying and death. (Feifel, 1963:12, also 11, 17)

Reeves suggests that the patient who is denied the truth has his manhood denied. "He is, in effect, dishonored and abandoned. And so he is likely to become embittered, self-pitying and complaining. . . ." (Reeves, 1969:5-9)

Contrary to the myth that a person should not be told of his terminal condition, it would appear that most patients and nonpatients want to be told of their condition and that the sharing of such information in a tactful, supportive manner can be of emotional benefit in helping most people to die with dignity.

VI.   Myth conception: Children cannot comprehend death.

Freud has said that death means little more to a child than departure or journey, and that if fear of death was evidenced, it was expected to appear after the oedipal period and is to be explained as a symbolic product of the fear of castration. (Freud, 1925:228-317)

C. W. Wahl says that " . . . the assertion, maintained even by professional persons, that children cannot conceive in any form of death, and hence, do not need to be reassured about it" is an adult defense to avoid coping with those anxieties in children. (Wahl, 1959:16-29) The fact that the child does not have an adult understanding of death does not mean that he has no understanding of it. Any understanding he does have is real to him, however different or distorted by adult standards, and is consequently real in its consequences.

Futterman and Hoffman in working with families with leukemic children found that most of the parents tended to believe the children, regardless of age, were oblivious to the fatal prognosis of leukemia. (Futterman and Hoffman, 1970:23-24) They indicate, however, that such a belief is a myth that protects the parents more than the child and may actually have harmful isolating effects on the child. In spite of the "delicate adaptational equilibrium" that such a myth maintains, Futterman and Hoffman "have become convinced of the need to risk upsetting the balance by challenging the notion that children are too young to understand. . . ." (Futterman and Hoffman, 1970:23-24)

Kliman points out that even though a child before the age of ten does not have a very extensive understanding of death, there are many things he does perceive. (Kliman, 1969:20-27) The child, for example, is quick to notice changes in behavior toward him, especially if loved ones seem to be keeping a secret from him. Kliman hints that even as our belief in the ignorance of children on sexual matters has changed, so will our beliefs about the ignorance of children on death change.

Arthur Carr points out that loss and separation are recurring themes of human existence and that from the time of birth, the growing child has constant experiences with losses that prepare him for death losses. (Carr, 1969:14-18) In spite of such loss experiences very little formal preparation for grief or understanding death occurs. Budmen states that most of a child's education is for life, which leaves him helpless in dealing with death. Such neglect he feels is inexcusable and unnecessary. (Budmen, 1969:11-12)

As attention is given to the identification of myth conceptions such as these, the taboo associated with death should be reduced. Our understanding of death and our ability to cope with death adequately should accordingly increase.

REFERENCES

Beecher, H. K., et al.
    1968   "A Definition of Irreversible Coma. Report of Ad Hoc Committee, Harvard Medical School, to Examine the Definition of Brain Death," J. Am. Med. Assoc., 205, 337.

Bromberg, W., and P. Schilder
  1933   "Death and Dying: A Comparative Study of the Attitudes and Mental
         Reactions Toward Death and Dying." Psychoanal. Review, 20: 133-
         185.

Budmen, K. O.
  1969   "Grief and the Young: A Need to Know." Arch. Foundation of Thana-
         tology, 1 (1): 11-12.

Cappon, D.
  1959   "The Dying." Psychiat. Quart., 33: 466-489.

Carlozzi, M.
  1970   "Must Death Be Final?" Arch. Foundation of Thanatology, 2 (1): 27.

Carr, A. C.
  1969   "A Lifetime of Preparation for Bereavement." Arch. Foundation of
         Thanatology, 1 (1): 14-18.

Feifel, H.
  1963   "Death." In Farberow, N. L., ed., Taboo Topics. New York: Ather-
         ton Press, p. 12. Also p. 11, 17.

Feifel, H., S. Hanson, R. Jones, and L. Edwards
  1967   "Physicians Consider Death." Proc. 75th Annual Convention, Amer.
         Psychol. Assoc., pp. 201-202.

Frankl, V. E.
  1959   From Death-Camp to Existentialism: A Psychiatrist's Path to a New
         Therapy, trans. by Ilse Lasch. Boston: Beacon Press.

Freud, S.
  1918   Reflections on War and Death. New York: Moffat, Yard & Co.

  1925   "Thoughts for the Times on War and Death." In Collected Papers.
         London: Hogarth Press, vol. 4: 228-317.

Futterman, E. H., and I. Hoffman
  1970   "Shielding from Awareness: An Aspect of Family Adaptation to Fatal
         Illness in Children." Arch. Foundation of Thanatology, 2 (1): 23-24.

14

Glaser, B., and A. Strauss
1965   Awareness of Dying. Chicago: Aldine Publishing Co.

Gorer, G.
1967   Death, Grief, and Mourning. Garden City, N.Y.: Doubleday & Co.,
        Anchor Books.

Hartland, E. S.
1928   "Death and Disposal of the Dead." Encyclopedia of Religion and Ethics,
        vol. 4. New York: Charles Scribner's Sons: 411-444.

Hinton, J.
1967   Dying. Baltimore: Penguin Books.

Jung, C. G.
1959   "The Soul and Death." In Feifel, H., ed., The Meaning of Death. New
        York: McGraw-Hill Book Co.: 3-15.

Kalish, R. A.
1965   "The Aged and the Dying Process: The Inevitable Decisions." J. of
        Social Issues, 21: 87-96 (95).

1966   "Life and Death: Dividing the Indivisible." Paper presented before the
        American Psychological Association, September, p. 3.

Kasper, A. M.
1959   "The Doctor and Death." In Feifel, H., ed., The Meaning of Death.
        New York: McGraw-Hill Book Co.: 259-270. Also p. 17.

Kastenbaum, R.
1969   "Death and Bereavement in Later Life." In Kutscher, A. H., ed.,
        Death and Bereavement. Springfield, Ill.: Charles C. Thomas Pub-
        lishers: 28-54 (31).

Knight, J. A., and F. Herter
1969   "Anticipatory Grief." In Kutscher, A. H., ed., Death and Bereavement.
        Springfield, Ill.: Charles C. Thomas Publishers: 196-201.

Kliman, G.
1969   "The Child Faces His Own Death." In Kutscher, A. H., ed., Death
        and Bereavement. Springfield, Ill.: Charles C. Thomas Publishers:
        20-27.

15

Lee, D.
1959   Freedom and Culture. Englewood Cliffs, N.J.: Prentice-Hall, Inc.

Malinowski, B.
1926   Crime and Custom in Savage Society. Garden City, N.Y.: Routledge, Inc.

Mayer, M.
1965   "On Death." In Hutchins, R. M., and M. J. Adler, eds., The Great Ideas Today. Chicago: Encyclopedia Britannica, Inc.: 107-164.

Oraison, M.
1969   Death--And Then What? Trans. by T. Du Bois. Paramus, N.J.: Paulist/Newman Press.

Reeves, R. B., Jr.
1969   "To Tell or Not to Tell the Patient." In Kutscher, A. H., ed., Death and Bereavement. Springfield, Ill.: Charles C. Thomas Publishers: 5-9.

Rosenberg, B., I. Gerver, and F. W. Howton
1964   Mass Society in Crisis. New York: The Macmillan Co.

Rosner, F.
1969   "The Definition of Death." Arch. Foundation of Thanatology, 1 (3): 105.

Schneidman, E.
1963   "Orientations Toward Death: A Vital Aspect of the Study of Lives." In White, R. W., ed., The Study of Lives. New York: Atherton Press: 201-227.

Shield, R.
1966   "Death and Dying: Attitudes of Patient and Doctor." New Haven (Conn.) Register, Jan. 20: 17.

Sorenson, J. L.
1956   "A Cultural Analysis of Some Recent American Funerals." Unpublished.

Stern, A.
1956   "Science and the Philosophers." American Scientist, 64: 291.

Still, J. W.
   1970   "We Need to Know Not Only When Human Life Ends but Even More
          Important, When It Begins." Arch. Foundation of Thanatology, 2 (2):
          66-74.

Stringfellow, W.
   1963   Instead of Death. New York: The Seabury Press, Inc.

Sumner, W. G., and A. C. Keller
   1927   The Science of Society. New Haven: Yale University Press.

Vernon, G. M.
   1970   Sociology of Death: An Analysis of Death-Related Behavior. New York:
          The Ronald Press Co.

Vrijhof, P. H.
   1967   "What Is the Sociology of Religion?" In Brothers, J., ed., Readings in
          the Sociology of Religion. New York: Pergamon Press, Inc.: 29-60
          (45).

Wahl, C. W.
   1959   "The Fear of Death." In Feifel, H., ed., The Meaning of Death. New
          York: McGraw-Hill Book Co.: 16-29.

Weisman, A. D., and T. P. Hackett
   1961   "Predilection to Death." Psychosomatic Medicine, 23: 323-356. Re-
          printed in Fulton, R., ed., Death and Identity. New York: John Wiley
          & Sons, Inc., 1965: 293-329 (317).

   1967   "Denial as a Social Act." In Levin, S., and R. J. Kanaha, eds., Psy-
          chodynamic Studies on Aging. New York: Internat. Universities Press,
          Inc.: 79-110.

CHAPTER 3

MYTH-CONCEPTIONS CONCERNING DEATH-RELATED BEHAVIOR

Glenn M. Vernon

Death-related behavior has become an area of considerable
interest to many, including those such as clergymen who confront
death as professionals and those such as sociologists who study
aspects of such behavior including the behavior of these professionals. This article is written to discuss some of the
myths which those who study death-related behavior have identified
in such study.

Disclosing a belief as a myth has mixed consequences. To
do so may help in the achievement of certain goals, but may in
the process create other goal-related problems. Not everyone
is seeking truth in all problem areas. With reference to death-
related behavior some may desire peace of mind and contentment
more than the knowledge that they are working with truth. In
decisions about how people confronting death will behave, knowing
an abstract truth is only part of the procedure. Decisions have
to be made about what one will do about that truth. These "what-
to-do" questions have no absolute abstract truth component, and
hence no "myth component." They are created by humans from the
experiences they have had.

A sociological analysis such as this one, starts with the
premise that determining truth is an important undertaking and
the hope that such knowledge may be useful. It is, of course,
"sociological truth" in which the sociologist is interested.
Criteria of such truthfulness is twofold: (1) where possible it
is based upon empirical evidence and (2) it harmonizes with
established theory. Symbolic interaction theory will be used in
this analysis. (See Vernon, 1970) Other types of truths exist
and knowing them may be very useful for other purposes.

                Abstract and Applied "Truths"

Statements about death and dying are frequently presented
as abstract truths or as statements with no qualifiers. As such,
they seem to be absolute and eternal. "Living is always preferable to dying" is such a statement. Included in that simple
statement are all types of living, all types of dying, and all
types of preferability or morality definitions. Further there
is the implicit assumption that we can distinguish life from
death and even the more basic assumption that living and dying

Vernon, Glenn M., 1970. Sociology of Death. New York:
   Ronald Press

18

are in fact separate entities or conditions, and that all possible preferences are known. The fact that "living" and "dying" are identified in the statement with separate labels implies separate entities. In such statements, it is as though the "truth" involved exists in some non-human state or in some "pure" state "uncontaminated" by humans.

While statements can be analyzed as though they did in fact exist in the state just described, when they are introduced into on-going behavior and applied to that behavior, they lose such abstractness, and the absoluteness, or eternalness associated therewith. They are applied abstracts. Applied statements fit into the ISAS paradigm (derived from the Symbolic Interaction perspective) with its four "relatives"--behavior of an individual (including decisions of an individual) are relative to symbols or meaning, to the audience(s) and the situation (See Vernon, 1970). Human behavior is much too complex, the elements involved are much too multidimensional and applications of evaluative words is much too human to permit of the stability and predictability implied in these abstract myths.

What is presented here in our analysis of myths is the types of qualifiers or "relativizers" which lead to questioning the abstract "truths."

Humans are both slaves to and masters over their symbols. Questioning established "facts" or "truths" and suggesting that they may in fact be myths is a part of the social movement in which established death taboos, to which we have been slaves, are being loosened. In effect the presentation here is an effort to become the master of our symbols and to change the relevant beliefs.

Previous Analysis

A previous article with Payne (See Vernon and Payne) identified and discussed the following myths:

1. An individual cannot conceive of his own death.
2. The meaning of life is death.
3. Death is a clearly defined phenomenon.
4. There is a biologically-given instinct for selv-preservation.
5. A dying person should not be told he is dying.
6. Children cannot comprehend death.

This article adds to and extends that discussion.

Vernon, Glenn M. and William D. Payne, 1975. Myth-Conceptions about Death. Journal of Religion and Health, Vol. 2, January, pp. 63-76.

Death-Related Myth-Conceptions

MYTH-CONCEPTION #1   LIVING IS ALWAYS PREFERABLE TO DYING

That this is a myth is suggested by the negative answer usually given to the question "Would you be willing to do just anything to preserve your own life?" In order to save yourself would you, for instance, permit the death of your child, your spouse, your church, your country? Would you refuse to serve in the military service in what you consider to be a moral cause? If you believed that God had appeared to you and provided you with some special revelation would you deny having had such an experience in order to save your life?

Preferable for whom--the one dying or the society? The problems of accepting the statement at face value are suggested by the fact that in our society

> We refuse to let some people die who want to
> die (who have decided that for them living
> is not preferable to dying),

BUT

> We insist upon taking the lives of some who
> wish to live or who accept the premise that
> living is preferable to dying.

Rejection of the statement is also implicit in the acceptance of the Christian statement (which non-Christians may reject) that greater love hath no one save he give his life for others, and in the Christian belief that Christ set the example by giving his life for the eternal well-being of humanity. Further, in the Eden Story of the "humanizing" of Eve and Adam, this first couple apparently voluntarily decided upon living a life which would terminate in death rather than living for eternity in the Garden. Acceptance of any of these beliefs rejects the myth.

Apparently, for many at least, certain types of dying are at times preferable to certain types of living.

MYTH-CONCEPTION #2   IT IS POSSIBLE FOR PEOPLE NOT TO "PLAY GOD"

The statement in which humans are told not to "play God" carries with it the implication that it is possible for them to do what they are being told not to do. "Playing God" in this case is defined as influencing established biological processes. Humans cannot not influence established biological processes. Without instincts, humans in fact have to influence biology to stay alive. The statement that humans should not "play God" is

20

typically made concerning those who do something to shorten the "living time" at the terminal period of living. However, if "tampering" with biology at this time is "playing God", such behavior at other times would logically also be "playing God." Influencing established biological processes is a life-long process. The entire lifetime experience of an individual "plays God" or influences the biological dying of a person. A complex set of interrelated societal variables influences any death.

If those who decrease the length of life are playing God, those who increase the length of life are also. But they don't say so. They never get accused of "playing God."

This myth seems to involve the untenable assumption that somehow the human biology could function and could "run down" without any socio-symbolic influences. This is impossible. Any human biological organism functions in some setting and is always influenced by human and nonhuman factors. It just might be, in fact, that in the human equivalent of a "vacuum" or without socio-symbolic influences the human biological machine would run forever. Who knows?

Actually, humans don't live in a vacuum. Biology doesn't function in a vacuum. Some, however, want to label the inevitable human input as non-human, or as "playing God." There is obviously a scapegoating potential involved. A question worth considering when "playing God" charges are introduced, is what motives are involved. Those who make the "don't play God" statements seem to be saying:

> "Don't influence biology if you interfere with my goals" which turns out to be a "don't interfere with me" statement. They may be more concerned with themselves than with the person dying.

> "Do influence biology even though it interferes with your goals."

The "playing God" charge implies that this is something which humans should avoid. However, if it is believed that the Lord does not intend for us to interfere with biological processes, how then can we justify interfering with the progress of disease that may lead to death, or using anesthesia for operations, or even performing operations in the first place? Why would anyone want NOT to influence biology?

The "don't play God" orientation seems to accept the premise that the time of death for a given individual is somehow pre-determined. They may believe that, as is stated in Ecclesiastes 3:1-2, that for everything there is a season—a time to be born and a time to die. The meaning of such a statement, however, varies if the time involved is "event time" rather than a mechanical clock-time system. In an event-time system one's time is up when he dies. In the clock-time system, one dies when his time is up.

MYTH-CONCEPTION #3   WE CAN BE SURE THAT WHAT HAPPENS BIOLOGICALLY
IS WILLED BY GOD--GOD SPEAKS TO US ONLY THRU OUR BIOLOGY

A contrary statement is that the "glory of God is intelligence," which implies that the will of God is expressed thru an
intelligent decision-making process. The Eden Story suggests
that Eve and Adam became human and "as the Gods" by learning how
to make moral decisions or how to utilize definitions of good and
evil. Potential cross-pressuring is involved. Is it the human
biology or the human intellect which expresses the will of God?

There is a meaningful distinction between a biological condition and what one does about that condition. The biology has
to be labeled in order for an individual-level (as contrasted
with an internal) response to be made. In behavior there are
then two basic components--the biological and the intellectual
involved in the labeling or making meaningful the biological.
There is then the question of how the biological "voice of God"
or what happens biologically, and the symboled "voice of God"
or what happens intellectually or symbolically, are interrelated.
When dissonance occurs, which neutralizes which? And then there
is the overriding question of whether what is happening is the
voice of God or the voice of humans.

There is further the question which related to Myth #2 of
whether it is in fact possible for humans NOT to interfere with
or influence biology.

It appears with reference to the "God-causes" involved that
a widely adopted practice obtains. When in explaining behavior
known or already realized non-God causes have been exhausted, we
fill in the gaps with religious or supernatural causes. When
humans did not understand how twins could be born, they were
viewed as being caused by God. When earthquakes were not
scientifically understood, a similar God-cause was used to provide
an acceptable explanation. When biological causes of death were
not well understood, God-causes were used to tidy up the explanation. Explanations about internal "God-causes" have also been
generalized to external causes. The individual who dies in an
auto accident then is seen as dying at the convenience of God,
or the death is viewed as God caused. This means that the
accident was God caused and God then becomes the responsible
agent for causing the accident, and the drunken driver, say, is
in effect relieved of responsibility.

Such an interpretation in effect, deifies biology or makes
a God of biology. Some at least would prefer to elevate the
intellect to the top level and believe that God speaks to humans
through our intellect.

MYTH-CONCEPTION #4   DYING OCCURS ONLY AT ONE POINT IN TIME--AT
THE END OF THE "TERMINAL PERIOD." DEATH IS CAUSED BY WHAT HAPPENS
IMMEDIATELY BEFORE THE LIVING STOPS

22

This myth ignores the point that what happens during the "terminal period" is only one small straw, which may have broken the camel's back (life) but was certainly not the entire load of straws which cumulatively produced the weight which terminated living.

As has been pointed out elsewhere (See Vernon, 1976) the somewhat trite statement that from the beginning of life an individual is in the process of dying has relevant meaning for our analysis. From the beginning of life, all human experiences have a relationship to or an impact upon the dying component of living. It would, in fact, be more accurate to use the label "living-dying experiences," than just "living experiences." Life expectancy is constantly being shortened by many living factors. One death-hastening factor is added to another and to another until the totality of death-creating or death-hastening factors outweigh the life-extending factors. At that time the individual dies biologically. The "death-straw" which "breaks the back" or terminates the life is but the last one added to many preceding ones. No one single straw causes the death or is the single death-causing factor.

Societal concern, however, has been focused much more extensively upon the terminal period and hence upon that "last straw than upon the gradually accumulating components (the stack of straws) and has contributed to the conclusion that everything possible should be done to extend the terminal stage. Such justification for the terminal extension, however, is frequently presented in a universal rather than an applied, time-limited perspective--everyone should always do everything possible to extend all or any life. "Life" is, of course, something that is involved from conception on, and the terminal life is viewed or interpreted as though it were the same as the pre-terminal living. The justification statements make no distinction between types of living or living at different periods of the life span. Hence, it is concluded that there is no such thing as "life" not worth living.

Such conclusions rest upon the assumption that the decision makers know what life is and conversely what death is and thus when death occurs or when dying takes place. As has been suggested, a label incorporating both life and death components might be more accurate and useful for some purposes. The relationship of living and dying can be pictured as follows:

The terminal person is dying as well as living and is living as well as dying. Treatment which prolongs life can also prolong death or dying. A meaningful question with reference to the dying/living ratio is whether there is a point at which the death-dying component should become the major focus of concern. Does the prolonging of life with a preponderance of dying behavior, justify prolonging the dying and delaying the death with its limited life components? Is there a point at which major concern should be with helping a person die with dignity which would typically include dying with a minimum of pain and suffering? If the answer is "yes" then attention should also be given to the fact that there are different types of pain and suffering. Pain related to a damaged self-image can be more difficult and intense than pain related to a damaged liver.

Do the living have any obligation to help a person have a good dying experience? Should just any type of dying be equally accepted and encouraged?

MYTH-CONCEPTION #5   "DEATH" OR "DEAD" ARE MORE ACCURATE LABELS THAN "PASSED ON"

In the general literature and in the accumulated writings of social-behavioral scientists in this area, one frequently encounters the idea that contemporary persons are reluctant to look at or to confront death directly. The real meaning of death is suppressed. People use euphemisms, screens or misleading, inaccurate labels to refer to death. Thus to use labels such as "passed on" rather than "dead" or "terminally ill" rather than "dying" is by implication wrong. These substitute labels do not provide the real meaning of death.

Any name or label and all meaning associated with a name is socially constructed. Any given label reflects some value premises. This is true of objective, scientifically usable names. Those who opt for "dead" may be attempting to get rid of religious interpretations which they themselves cannot accept, but attempting to do so in what appears to many to be non-religious or non-faith ways, or for non-religious reasons.

When people name or label something they do not stop with just that. People have no abstract "naming drive." We name for a purpose and that purpose, whatever it is, gets involved in the meaning associated with the name. We are concerned not only with "it is" but also with how we relate to it or what we do about it. The question as to what it is empirically can be answered scientifically. "What do we do about it?" cannot. There is then no universal, absolute criteria of what is a myth and what is not a myth with reference to "what to do" criteria or decisions.

Some, the immortalists, believe that there is a life
after death. The anti-immortalists believe that there is
nothing after death. Death is the end. Both of these are
faith-type beliefs. Neither is a scientific fact. Both the
immortalists and the anti-immortalists accept the scientific
facts about biological death. They do not question these.
The difference concerns the post-death condition on which
there is no scientific truth one way or another.

It is a myth that one set of labels is more accurate than
the other. Each reflects the religious convictions of those
involved.

MYTH-CONCEPTION #6 PERSONS WHO ARE DYING KNOW WITHOUT BEING
TOLD THAT THEY ARE DYING

This myth rests upon the assumption that dying is a
recognizable condition, as contrasted with living, rather than
a "ratio-ed" configuration.

It is surprising that physicians and nurses who are
accustomed to having persons come to them to have the experts
tell them what their biology means, at this terminal point deny
or negate their "expert" role and state that at this stage the
biology in effect takes over and informs the person that he is
dying.

The myth ignores the whole symbolic interaction perspective
that behavior which takes biology into account is in response
to symbols. There is in fact no meaning in biology. Humans
have to symbol such meaning into existence so that they can tell
themselves what the biology means. Whatever they do will be in
response to the meaning--not the biology.

It is interesting that those who profess to believe that
the person automatically knows that he is dying, never seem to
get around to telling us how such knowledge is known. They also
never seem to say much about how many have thought they were
dying when they were not.

Also they never get around to considering why the experts,
i.e., the physicians, can at times make mistakes and conclude
that a person is going to die when he does not die. How can
they conclude that the dying person somehow has an infallible
"death-detector" built in?

One thing which happens is that the physician or medical
personnel can conclude that the person knows and thus the medical
personnel never give concern to what might be the consequences
of not knowing but suspecting. The agony of uncertainty can be
overlooked or ignored.

There is a difference between knowing that something is happening biologically and knowing that I am dying. Each person living is dying. We know this however because we have learned it, not because our biology somehow tells each of us.

MYTH-CONCEPTION #7   BIOLOGICAL DEATH IS THE MAJOR THING (OR THE MOST IMPORTANT THING) WHICH IS HAPPENING WHEN A PERSON DIES?

We have a long history of evaluating biological factors as of greater value than symbol-meaning factors. This myth perpetuates this perspective.

In the area of death-related behavior, we can distinguish death at each of the following levels:

A. Biological death or what happens when the biological "machine" stops functioning. We are not nearly as sure today as we used to be that we know when this type of death occurs.

B. Social or interactional death which occurs when established behavior patterns or interaction patterns are destroyed or "killed." Such death occurs when one individual or a group of individuals are no longer able to do what they used to do, or to engage in previously available behavior. The label "death" seems to be appropriate because of the literal destruction involved. What once was, is no longer in existence and further is incapable of being "resurrected" or re-created.

C. Symbolic death, the neutralization or destruction of symbols. Names or labels are destroyed. Identity symbols or identity documents are important to most of us. Preserving them intact or enhancing them is usually important. Destruction thereof can be extremely difficult, as in the case of Spiro Agnew losing his title of United States Vice President with its accompanying position.

An important point which is frequently overlooked in discussions of biological death, is that death at all three levels is involved. The one dying experiences biological death. His experience of that process (the awareness of which is symbolic as contrasted with the actual biological death) is related to what others communicate to him. Experts or significant others play a crucial role in such awareness. Social or relationship death inevitably follows biological death. Symbolic death may also be involved.

Characteristics of Social Death

A social death, or the death of a relationship takes place when the possibility of engaging in that particular relationship no longer exists. When two individuals who have related to each other are no longer able to do so, the relationship has been destroyed. The concept of "relationship" being used here is inherently social in nature. It requires two (or more) individuals mutually taking each other into account. It is not an individual phenomenon. Both individuals are required or you don't have a relationship. The importance of relationships is emphasized from awareness that individuals spend most of their lives relating to others. Most behavior of one individual is intertwined with that of others. Individuals constantly tailor behavior to harmonize or mesh with that of others. The behavior of one individual is but one essential part of a relationship which requires another individual.

The relationship per se, and awareness of that relationship are two different things. Part of death adjustment involved for the living is changing these symbols to take into account the relationship which is dying or dead. Meaning has to be changed. Labels have to be changed.

Kubler-Rose (1969) identified the following stages involved in the acceptance by the person dying that he is in fact dying: denial, anger, bargaining, depression and acceptance. It is likely that variations of the same stages are involved in acceptance of the fact that a relationship is dying or being destroyed.

A largely ignored fact, is that those in the pre-bereavement stage are also experiencing a type of death--i.e., social death. They are working through the process by which established behavior patterns are very literally being destroyed. Previous behavior with the one biologically dying usually experiences deterioration and change, especially if hospitalization is involved and physical interaction is reduced, restricted or maybe eliminated. In any event, as the one dying approaches death, his loved ones are typically aware of the impending biological death, and of the impending interactional or social death as well.

Behavior at the individual level is in response to symbols. From this perspective the behavioral death may be equally or more difficult to experience for those experiencing this type of death than the biological death for the one experiencing that death. Such individuals, however, are not often treated as though they were involved in a death process. Greater attention given to this fact by their significant others might serve to reduce the trauma of such a death experience.

The person experiencing biological death is frequently likewise caught up in the behavior death. He usually is aware that

Kubler-Ross, Elizabeth, 1969. On Death and Dying. New York: The Macmillan Company

he is no longer able to sustain, initiate or experience previously enjoyed behavior. He can no longer relate to others as he did previously.

It also at times happens that he experiences behavior death before he experiences biological death. When family members cease to and maybe refuse to visit him, or maintain any type of symbolic contact via letters, telephone calls, etc., he gradually learns to accept the verdict of relationship death. His relationships have literally been destroyed. He is no longer able to do what he used to. He has, in effect, experienced a behavioral amputation. Part of his previous behavior is dead.

To undergo such an experience can be traumatic, and may very well make a heavy contribution to the subsequent biological death. One typically does not live long when there is nothing for which he wants to live.

Summary

The discussion here has suggested that it is likely that the following beliefs are myth conceptions:

Living is always preferable to dying.
It is possible for people not to "play God."
We can be sure that what happens biologically is willed by God. God speaks to us only thru our biology.
Dying occurs only at one point in time--at the end of the "terminal period."
"Death" or "Dead" are more accurate labels than "passed on."
Persons who are dying know without being told that they are dying.
Biological death is the most important thing which is happening when a person dies.

The goal of achieving understanding of our death-related behavior can be facilitated by recognition of the myth-conceptions such as these and the previously identified myths the acceptance of which may have an impact upon both biological and mental or spiritual health of those involved.

CHAPTER 4

DYING AS A SOCIAL-SYMBOLIC PROCESS

GLENN M. VERNON

The increased attention currently being given to the study of death-
related behavior or what some have called thanatology has been the impetus
for changing interpretations of death and the expansion of certain perspectives and types of awareness. This article is an outgrowth of several
years of participation in this movement involving analysis of death-related
behavior utilizing concepts and orientations which are a part of a
perspecitve called Symbolic Interactionism. The basic perspective of
symbolic interactionism is that the behavior of the individual is in response
to symbols (meaning, knowledge, etc.) and is relative to the audience and
the situation, which is expressed in paradigm manner as ISAS.[1] This
perspective then places strong emphasis upon both the social and the symbolic
nature of human interaction.

This article presents some of the insights which have developed from
this analysis which focuses attention primarily upon the social-symbolic
dimensions rather than the biological aspects of dying. We thus make a
distinction between (a) biological death, (b) social death and (c) symbolic
death, which are interrelated by distinguishable phenomena.

Biological Death and Social-Symbolic Death

Death has many related aspects. Clearly death involves biology, and
the initial definitions or conceptions utilized by most people when they
hear the word "death" are primarily biological in nature. However, social
scientists in some respects and our general society to a much less extent,
have started to add to the awareness of biological components of death,
awareness of the social and the symbolic components. Doing so and concentrating
study upon the social-symbolic aspects leads one to a perspective of an to
an understanding of death, quite different from that derived from a focus
upon the biological components. The act of dying biologically is at the
same time very much both social and symbolic in nature. The profound significance to this fact, which seems to have escaped the attention of many,
almost seems to justify the conclusion that dying is more of a social-
symbolic act than a biological act.

If by "death" one means a biological change, the social scientist
really isn't studying death at all. What the social scientist studies is
behavior related to biological death. Such death related behavior has two
major characteristics: (1) it is social or interactional in nature and (2)
it is symbolic in nature with each of these characteristics being an integral
aspect of the other. Human social interaction is symbolic interaction, and
human symbols are by their very nature social.

---

[1] For a further discussion of the ISAS paradigm see Glenn M. Vernon
Human Interaction (New York: Ronald Press, 2nd ed., 1972).

A symbol is something which stands for or represents (re-presents) something else. There are then in effect two types of "bodies" or two types of phenomenon involved in behavior: (a) the biological body and (b) the symbols which re-present that body. The "symbolic body" consists of all of the definitions, knowledge, beliefs, evaluations, ect., which are related to the biological body. What an individual does about his biological body is in response to symbols or the symbolic body. He responds to the meaning not the actual biological body. This is equally true of all behavior of the individual, which is in response to symbols, not to the raw unidentified world per se.

As social scientists we really have little if any legitimate interest in the process which is of major concern to the biological expert, i.e., the process by which the heart stops beating, or the brain stops functioning. These are processes which go on inside the individual. Neither of these is individual-level phenomenon. We are concerned, however, with the process by which "the individual" dies. An individual is composed of more than one organ, any one of which can now, or most likely will, be capable of being replaced by transplant, or of having a machine substitute provided. It is the individual as he related to other individuals with which we are concerned. We are concerned with the meaning of a stopped heart or a non-functioning brain, but not with the heart or brain per se. The basic human practice of providing or creating meaning is something an individual does, not something the brain or some other internal biological entity does. The individual who is dying typically struggles with the meaning of dying as well as with the biolgocial process of dying.

The biological process of dying takes place conjointly with the social-symbolic process of dying. The relationships between these two factors are two-way rather than one-way. To focus attention primarily upon the biological process ignores the very important social-symbolic process. Dying has many causes. The social factors are easily identifiable in a capital punishment death which takes place in the death chamber in which representatives of society decide when, where, how and how quickly the biological death is achieved. While not so apparent or manifest, similar social factors can be identified for almost all deaths, including deaths related to over-pollution, war, poorly designed highways and cars, smoking, playing football and other sports, mountain climbing, poor diet, lack of medical expertise and medical facilities including life-saving machines, and living "the pace that kills."

The death of the individual is caused every bit as much by the social-symbolic factors as by the biological entities inside.

It is true that there is a human build-in obsolescence. Every human being will eventually and inevitably die. His biology will eventually run down. However, this eventual inevitable death never occurs. Biological factors alone are never given such a "free reign." Social-symbolic factors always influence the actual death. Thus we can distinguish between (1) inevitable eventual death and (2) pre-inevitable death which stems from social-symbolic factors. The pre-inevitable death occurs when the social-symbolic "stage" is set for it to happen.

Many would say that biological death should be the starting point for any discussion concerning death, since the social-symbolic factors only accompany or are subsidiary to the biological death which occurs. However, it is just as accurate to use as the starting point, the social-symbolic factors which bring the biological body to its dying point, hastening or delaying the biological death according to the configuration of social-symbolic variables involved. Biological death is universal and inevitable. For humans, the social-symbolic factors are species-specific factors which are likewise universal and inevitable post-natal phenomena.

We will now turn our attention to the use of the perspective we have developed in an analysis of several aspects of dying.

Who Owns the Biological Body and
Who Owns the Symbolic Body

An intriguing question found in the literature which has all sorts of implications for decisions about death is "who owns my body?" The signficant spin-off question is who makes decisions about what happens to my body. Or who should be legitimated or approved to make decisions about my body. Such questions and the related answers focus upon the biological body, which of course in where biological death takes place.

The question re-stated with emphasis upon the social and symbolic nature of behavior is "who owns my symbolic body?" which includes some variation of the following:

1. Who owns my name-symbols?
2. Who owns the definitions of me?
3. Of what symbolic entities are my identifications a part?
4. To which group names does my name belong.

The answer to these is basically that the set of symbols which represent me is a part of many group names or of many symbolic entities. The biological individual is a separate biological entity with clearly identifiable boundaries. There is no such thing as the integration or amalgamation of the biological individual into some larger biological entity. This same thing is not true, however, of the symbolic body. This body is symbolic and has much greater plasticity and flexibility than the biological body. Various names and related symbols can be integrated into an almost unlimited array of configurations each of which can be real-ized (made symbolically real) and taken into account.

From the symbolic interaction perspective, clearly many different groups "have a claim" upon my reputation or my name-symbols. I am a legitimate recognized part of a group, and my living-dying influences the symbolic entity including the self image of the group. The meaning of my death does influence the definitions of the groups to which I belong or of which I am a part. My death then is a matter of concern for those groups whose symbolic boundaries incorporate my name, such as the family, the professional group, the church, the community. My symbols are a legitimate part of such symbolic entities. From this perspective "my" symbols turn out not to be exclusively mine, but are rather shared social symbols. When one focuses attention not upon biology but upon symbols, the collective, group, or social nature of the symbols (not the bodies) is most evident.

When I die part of the group dies. When there is a change in my name-symbols, there is a corresponding change in the symbolic group entity. Part of it changes. The impact of any such change is related to the extent to which the symbols representing the individual are interwined with significant others in that symbolic entity.

31

"Who owns the biological me?" is an important question. Equally important,
however, is the question of who owns the symbolic me, or the symbols which
re-present the biological me.

Kubler-Ross Stages[2]

Dr. Elisabeth Kubler-Ross, from her experiences in working with such
individuals, identified five stages which she found to be characteristic of
the behavior of individuals as they became aware of the fact that they were
facing biological death. Analyzing these stages from the ISAS perspective
increases our understanding of what happens during each state and provides
some insights as to why the sequence occurs as it does. The stages are not
to be veiwed as applying to everyone, at least not in exactly the sequence
outlined. Five interrelated important aspects of accepting or real-izing
(making real) the fact that one is dying are however involved.

Denial. This first stage involves primarily the individual and his self-
defintions. In terms of the ISAS paradigm components this stage can be
characterized as I ⟲ Sy since the individual is his own audience as he
assesses the accuracy of applying particular labels to himself. This is the
stage in which the individual works through any problems or difficulties
associated with changing of the self defintion "I am living" or "I am
dying." The "I am living" definition which has been a "constant companion"
for many years has for some reason been challenged and the individual has
been told that he is dying. He most likely is told this by another person,
although this may be an aspect or illustration of self-generated awareness
in which the same individual is his own audience. That there is an initial
denial of such possible changed definitions is no surprise for individuals
who highly evaluate living. For some, however, this awareness may be accepted
with thankfulness. Kubler-Ross worked primarily with those who were in the
denial categories.

The desire of many people to seek isolation from others at this time
is no surprise. Changing such crucial self definitions may be something
they want to work through themselves. Such an individual must somehow
neutralize the "I am living" component of his self image and substitute
an "I am dying" component in its place. This requires some significant
symbolic shifting and maneuvering. Dying individuals want to think about
the significance of such a change. They want to make a symbolic assessment
of what has happened in the past and give attention to pre-creating a future
with this new definition or self image incorporated therein.

This initial stage is, of course, an important aspect of the labeling
process in which the individual in effect "toys" with the applicability
of a certain label to himself. As is true of most highly evaluated labels,
and new label is not in some sponge-like manner, just passively accepted
and incorporated into the larger set of self definitions. The individual

---

[2] Elisabeth Kubler-Ross, One Death and Dying (New York: Macmillan, 1970).

is in effect negotiating with himself. He is his own audience. He is apparently assessing the evidence he has available to see if it justifies a change of labels. He in effect tries on the new label, checking its goodness of fit.

In such an assessment the initial interpretation of many is apparently one of denial. The "dying" label is rejected.

Anger-Bargaining Stages. These two stages follow in logical sequence from an acceptance of a label change. There would be little likelihood that they would come before the denial stage. Being angry or bargaining for a change of status makes sense only if the "I am dying" label or categorization has been at least partially accepted. If I agree that I am dying, then I may get angry about it. I believe it, but I don't like it. If I accept the fact that I am dying, I may attempt to do something about it by seeking outside help from whatever source I may consider to be appropriate, and it would include for many, both supernatural as well as natural audiences.

Anger is a negative reaction. I real-ize that I am dying but I don't like it. The fighting against it is primarily a symbolic phenomenon. I react by feeding into my definitions negative evaluations of whatever or who ever I see as being responsible for my changed condition. The anger may of course be self directed, if I somehow conclude that I am responsible for my dying condition. In this stage I can't just clamly accept the changed defintions. In the ISAS sequence or "space" this action is also at IS plus the ISA stage. In the bargaining stage, attention is focused outside the individual, and the inter-action or the I - A components of the paradigm are emphasized. This is a social process. Behavior is relative to the audience.

Bargaining involves acceptance of the new state or category but with the related conviction, maybe only partially but hopefully accepted, that possibly something can be done about reversing the definition. I may be dying, but I don't want to die. In fact, I refuse to die, and I need help in securing this goal. The audiences involved in such bargaining strategy may of course be myself, my physician, my nurse, my family, my God, my clergy-man or some other significant religious others. At least as is portrayed in literature, the bargaining may even involve negotiations with the devil, in which the individual agrees to sell his soul for a life-saving price.

When the bargaining phase is exhausted and acceptance achieved, or when the individual receives or real-izes a "no" answer to his pleas for help and assistance, he is ready to move to the next stage - depression.

Depression. Attention returns again at this state to self definitions, moving from I - A to I - Sy. Such definitions now clearly incorporate an "I am dying" component with a negative evaluation thereof. Yes, I'm dying, but I don't like being in this condition. The individual is depressed and unhappy about his condition. I don't like to be dying. I don't like myself as a dying person.

Significant others at this stage may through their behavior, words, or both, reinforce such definitions by one way or another communicating "we don't like you as a dying person." Your social status has changed as your biological status has changed. Such audience input can reinforce the depression. The reverse social input of "We like and accept you as a dying person," would in most cases facilitate and legitimate the creation of self-like and self acceptance. The negative audience input may incorporate a component of "We don't like ourselves or our situation-condition, as a result of your dying." Your death influences us since you are a part of us, and we don't like what is happening. Maybe you are deserting us; you are not available to provide the input you used to. The physician who defines a death as a professional failure on his part since he is supposed to preserve and protect life, may also directly or indirectly communicate to the dying individual the basic message that "I don't like you or approve of you as a dying person. Your dying is a threat to my self image since it proves that I failed to save a life in your case." This increases the likelihood that an individual may have problems liking himself in that stage.

Part of the "We don't like you as a dying person" may in fact be "We don't like ourselves with you in this category." The message communicated to the dying individual however, may be primarily focused upon the person dying. The problems of the bereaved get focused upon the dying individual. This may be easier for the "bereaving" but more difficult for the "deceasing."

Acceptance. The final stage, which may not be reached by all those who die, involves acceptance rather than denial. This, of course, is a symbolic component. The individual real-izes that change agents are not available, and that further bargaining would be of no avail. He concludes that being depressed for being sorry for oneself, serves no helpful purpose and thus, the individual accepts the "dying" label. At this stage a common reality base has been created for the individual and his audience. They all realize the same thing. They all know what is happening. They can then proceed with their interaction or with their living, operating from a common accepted frame of reference. As in most cases, complete consensus as to the reality involved in most likely never achieved. One last hope may be entertained until after the death has actually occurred, and maybe even beyond with the help of religious beliefs.

Situational Components of the ISAS Orientation

While the Ross stages do not call attention to the involvement of situational components in the developmental sequences we can hypothesize that situational factors are taken into account as validating or challenging factors. All of the behavior we have been discussing in the five stages takes place "on some stage" or in some situation. Situational factors then are bound to influence what takes place, possibly as accentuating or diminishing factors. The spatial location of the dying individual may serve to reinforce a "dying" definition. Movement from one section of the hospital to another, or from the hospital to the home may do so. Being placed in certain hospital sections in effect places the person in a "dying quarantine" which limits the individuals who may interact with him. Relating to a religious audience, such as in being given last rites, may also reinforce a dying definition.

In the process of dying, attention is gradually changed from phenomenon outside the individual to himself, especially his self definitions. He tries to understand what is happening to his biology inside of him. His lack of previous experiences such as this means that an ambiguous mysterious, component is most likely involved. He may conclude that no one else can know as he does what he is experiencing and thus disengage himself symbolically if not physically from established social contacts and from roles he has been playing in the past. After all, biological dying is one of the most individualistic things one can do. Searching for meaning cues from environmental-situational factors is a frequent occurrence.

34

Extending the Kubler-Ross Stages

Kubler-Ross focused her attention upon the stages involved in the dying individual's reactions to his own impending death. It appears that the reaction of an individual to the unwelcome impending death or in some cases the actual death of a significant other may also incorporate these basic components.

1. Denial of the fact that this other is dying.
2. Anger as a result of being "treated" in such a way, or in an empathetic sense, anger in behalf of or with the dying.
3. Bargaining with others or with the dying individual for the life of this signficant other.
4. Depression or sorrow at the impending loss of this other, with an empathic component of sharing depression with the dying.
5. Acceptance, which again involves or signifies the creation of a socially-constructed reality base from which future interaction occurs. Everyone real-izes the same thing.

Evaluation of Preserving Biological Life

We are beginning to question whether the widely-accepted value hierachy, which places biological preservation at the top of the hierarchy, is the one we really want to accept today. Maybe most people would accept this hierarchy as an abstract phenomenon not applied to any specific individual as he relates to particular audiences in particular situations. However, as far as actual applied evaluation-decisions are concerned, there are situation-audience-meaning configurations which lead most individuals to opt for some other highest-intensity priority such as dignified dying, or preservation of certain self definitions or family definitions. These symbolic components are given higher priority that the biological components. Behavior is relative to the situation. Over the years the typical dying situation has evidenced tremendous change.

Awareness that individuals in fact do evaluate symbolic phenomena as of greater importance than biological phenomena leads to a rejection of the belief that individuals come equipped with a biologically built-in biological-preservation instinct or drive, which functions to preserve life at the level of the individual as contrasted with a sub-individual level. At the individual level behavior stems from the decision made, or from symbolic phenomena, not from the biology.

One Leap of Faith-Two Differing Conclusions

Focusing attention upon symbolic-social aspects of death-related behavior makes one aware of the symbolic nature of the following two contrasting beliefs: (1) there is a life after death and (2) there is no life after death. Frequently the assumption is made that the first one is of a religious nature, involving faith-type answers and the second one is more scientific, empirical, logical, or rationally defensible. Actually, however, both decisions are faith type decision, and if one is religious the other is equally religious except that it may not involve any supernatural concept.

35

Empirical evidence leads us to the conclusion that an individual dies and that eventually the biological body decomposes. There is little if any agrument between the "life-after-death" people and the "no-life-after-death" people up to that point. Once you get beyond that point, however, any conclusion is a matter of faith or requires a symbolic leap or jump beyond the empirical evidence. If one interpretation is condemned for a lack of empirical evidence, the other stands equally condemned.

Either interpretation illustrates the importance of the human use of non-referented symbols which transcend or go beyond the empirical world, including the biological body. It is not a question of whether or not one will use faith based interpretation. The only meaningful question is what type of faith-based definitions will be accepted.

Symbolic and "Spiritual"

The SI theorist and most religionists share the fundamental belief or premise that there is something to being human in addition to the biological components. To the SI theorist this something else is symbolic. To the religionist it is spiritual. The religionist can incorporate the symbolic component into his larger configuration. The SI theorist cannot incorporate many of the basic components of the religionist's "something else" into his.

The relationship between these two types of phenomena merits study. How does that which the religionist calls "spiritual" relate to that which the symbolic interactionist calls "symbolic"?

Summary and Conclusions

This article has called attention to the fact that the study of death should be expanded to include not only the study of biological factors but the study of social and symbolic factors as well. It is maintained that if one desires to understand what individuals do about death, as contrasted with what the biology of the individual does, study encompassing both the social and the symbolic is essential. Without such attention, some basic characteristics of death are overlooked. Expanded understanding results when a distinction is made between biological death, social death and symbolic death. Answers to questions of ownership-control of the "body" differ if attention is focused upon the "symbolic body" rather than, or as well as, on the biological body.

The five stages of dying identified by Kubler-Ross are given expanded meaning if insights secured from an ISAS analysis are used. These stages may be used to analyze the reactions to the death of others as well.

Focusing attention upon the symbol-social aspects of death provides for a re-structured hierarchy of high intensity value definitions which places symbolic-social factors above biological factors. We have also emphasized that a life-after-death and a no-life-after-death interpretation are each equally grounded in the faith method since in each case movement beyond empirical-biological components is required. Man does not live by bread alone-neither does he die by bread alone. Both living and dying behavior are in response to symbols, relative to the audience and relative to the situation.

CHAPTER 5

DYING AS SOCIAL BEHAVIOR:
MORMON BEHAVIOR THROUGH HALF A CENTURY

Glenn M. Vernon
Charles E. Waddell

University of Utah

The personification of death as the lawless one, the one who strikes at random without regard to person, time, or situation, has long been recognized as a "folk-myth-conception" (1). Parallel with this notion of death personified, is the present widely-held belief that its inevitability makes death primarily biological in nature (2). However, as Coleman (3) discusses, contemporary medical technology has devised life-sustaining techniques to such a point that the actual occurrence of death is problematic.

It follows, however, that if contemporary medical technology (a social factor) influences death patterns, the equally social lack of medical technology in less contemporary societies influences death patterns. Biological death is inevitable, the actual death however whatever the social conditions is influenced by those social conditions.

In other words, death is much more than a biological phenomenon. An adequate analysis of death and dying has been hindered by the fact that the one concept "death" has been used to identify several different phenomena each of which is distinctly different from the others. Kalish (4) suggests that we remedy this situation by distinguishing five types of death: (1) biological, (2) clinical, (3) psychological, (4) social and (5) sociological.[1]

Using this typology we can then identify the different type or level of phenomenon involved in each type of death as follows:

Biological: Something which happens to the biology inside the individual.

Clinical: Something which happens at the individual level.

Psychological: Something which happens at the symbolic level-- i.e., the individual is no longer able to define himself.

Social: Something which happens at the micro sociosymbolic level-- i.e., individual is no longer able to relate to others in previously established ways. Interaction involving the individual and the community is no longer possible.

Rather than view death as an occurrence, Nyberg (5) suggests that it may be useful to view dying as a form of social behavior that is learned. In other words, at the individual/social level, not only do humans learn how to die (2) but they learn to die. Although Nyberg may be overstating the behavioral nature of death, exploring dying as a form of social behavior is fascinating. It is the purpose of this paper to partially explore this view of dying. Specifically, we compare the death rates of Mormons from 1929 to 1970 with the death rates of (1) other Americans and (2) Utah residents in an attempt to illustrate the social nature of dying.

Social Behavior. Social behavior may be viewed as behavior in response to symbols, relative to audience(s) and situation(s) which is capsulized as ISAS. (6) For example, research by Spicer and Gustavus (7) summarized in Figure 1 illustrates that birth behavior, another area which is also typically interpreted in biological terms, may be viewed as social behavior. That is, Mormon birth behavior is in response to pronatalist symbols[2] since the Mormon birth rate is higher than the United States or Utah birth rates. Simultaneously, the similarity in the variable patterns of birth rates among the three populations illustrates that Mormon birth behavior is relative to audience(s) and situation(s) of the larger culture. Since it evidences the same patterns, the death behavior of Mormons may be viewed in this same manner.

Figure 1
Birth Rates--Mormons, Utah and the United States: 1920-1969*

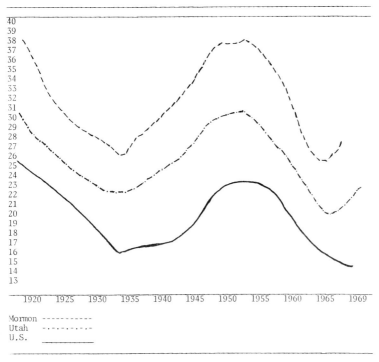

Mormon ----------
Utah   -..-..-..-.-
U.S.   _____

*Taken from "Mormon Fertility through Half a Century: a Test of the Americanization Hypothesis." Judith C. Spicer and Susan O. Gustavus, Social Biology, forthcoming.

The Mormons. The Church of Jesus Christ of Latter-day Saints, or the Mormon Church, is a religious group with a low death rate tradition. The state of Utah, site of the church headquarters, and with 72 percent of its population claimed by the Mormon Church in 1971, had the lowest death rate of any state in the continental United States in 1970 at 6.9 per 1,000 (8).[5] Table 1 shows the increasing percent of Mormons in Utah from 1910 to 1971 (Historical Department, Church of Jesus Christ of Latter-day Saints).

Table 1
Population of Utah and Percent of Utah Residents Claimed by
the Mormon Church: 1910-1971*

Year	Utah Population	% of Utah Mormon
1910	373,351	61
1920	449,396	60
1930	507,847	64
1940	550,310	64
1950	688,862	68
1960	891,000	72
1970	1,059,419	73
1971	1,095,000 (est.)	72

*Obtained from the Historical Department of the Church of Jesus Christ of Latter-day Saints.

The position of the Mormon Church on health-related matters is best illustrated by its "Word of Wisdom" (9). The "Word of Wisdom" emphasizes abstinence from alcohol, tobacco, and hot drinks as well as moderation in the eating of meat and the obligation to eat "wholesome foods."

Further, the emphasis on the "Word of Wisdom" among the Mormons is quite strong. A review of the Church's bi-annual conference reports between 1920 and 1970 (100 meetings) reveals that at each meeting the "Word of Wisdom" was one way or another the subject matter of sermons presented, indicating that the leadership of the church expected the members to live according to this standard. (Historical Department, Church of Jesus Christ of Latter-day Saints).

Table 2 shows that deaths due to heart-, cancer-, and liver-related diseases, three of the ten leading causes of death in America, which are somewhat related to smoking and drinking, are less prevalent in Utah than in the United States

Table 2
Death Rate per 100,000
due to
Heart-, Cancer-, Liver-, and Infancy-Related diseases and to Accidents for Utah
and the United States
1940, 1949, 1959 and 1968*

		Heart	Cancer	Liver	Infancy	Accidents
1940	U.S.	292.5	120.3	- - - -	49.2	- - - -
	Utah	344.6	91.0	- - - -	67.4	- - - -
1949	U.S.	349.1	138.9	- — -	43.2	60.7
	Utah	248.0	84.2	- - - -	52.1	70.9
1959	U.S.	363.4	147.4	10.9	38.5	52.2
	Utah	233.4	88.8	7.0	36.5	54.2
1968	U.S.	372.6	159.4	14.6	21.9	57.5
	Utah	226.2	88.7	7.8	22.7	55.9

- - - - Not given
* Statistical Abstracts, 1942, 1951, 1961, and 1970. These are
five of the ten leading causes of death in the United States.

generally. (8)[4] However, with respect to deaths by accidents and early infancy
diseases, there appears to be no significant differences between Utah and the
rest of the United States. Thus, it is argued that Mormon death behavior is
particularly in response to health-related symbols such as those in the "Word of
Wisdom."

Likewise, Vernon (9), in an availability sample of students throughout the
United States, compared Mormons with various non-Mormon groups on attitudes
toward death. From his analysis, the meanings of death endorsed by the Mormon
group are significantly different from those of other groups involved. Mormon
attitudes characteristically included a strong transcendental belief in a future
existence, and a strong wish to live after death and to experience a reunion
with loved ones in eternity. Of those studied, the Mormons were least likely
to worry about eternity and were most likely to specify that they would extensively change their life styles if they knew for sure there was no life
after death. Lastly, Mormons see their orientation towards death as being related to their religious experience. Thus, on the basis of these data it is
also argued that Mormon death behavior is in response to the distinctive death-
related symbols of their religious experience.

40

The Data. Mormon death rates between 1920 and 1970 were compared to Utah and United States death rates. The data on Mormon death rates were obtained from the Historical Department of the Church of Jesus Christ of Latter-Day Saints.

The death rates include world-wide Church membership. Information is not currently available for only the United States Mormons. However, the vast majority of the Mormon membership outside the United States is found in industrial nations with a strong western tradition (7).

The death rates of Utah and the United States were obtained from Statistical Abstracts of the United States, 1922 through 1972. Utah was chosen because of its high concentration of Mormons (see Table 1).

Results. Table 3 provides the death rates of Mormons, Utah residents, and the United States population at five-year intervals from 1920 to 1970. These data are presented graphically in Figure 2.

TABLE 3

DEATH RATES PER 1,000 - MORMONS, UTAH RESIDENTS, AND THE UNITED STATES POPULATION: 1920-1970

Year	Mormon*	Utah**	U. S.**
1920	9.0	11.5	13.0
1925	7.7	9.3	11.8
1930	7.6	9.9	11.3
1935	7.3	9.8	10.9
1940	6.5	8.9	10.8
1945	6.4	7.9	10.6
1950	6.0	6.8	9.6
1955	5.5	6.7	9.3
1960	5.3	6.8	9.5
1965	5.2	6.7	9.4
1970	4.8	6.9	9.4

*Historical Department, Church of Jesus Christ of Latter-Day Saints.

**Statistical Abstracts, 1922 through 1972.

41

Figure 2
Death Rates per 1,000--Mormons, Utah and the United States: 1920-1970

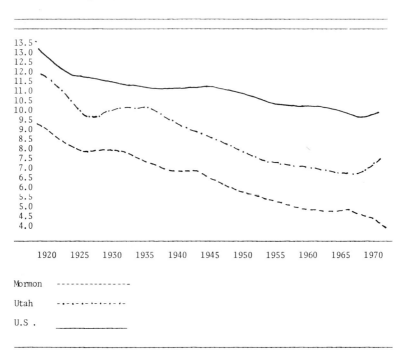

Mormon   ----------------

Utah   - -- .- .- .-.- . .- .-

U.S .   _____

It is clear that Mormons have a lower death rate throughout this period
than either total Utah residents or the population of the United States. While
this ordering of the three populations with regard to the level of the death
rates was expected, the very great similarity in the pattern of the death rate
among the three populations was rather surprising.

All three populations show a decline in the death rate from 1920 through
1970. However, throughout this decline the difference in the Mormon and U.S.
death rates has been remarkably stable. In 1920, this difference was 4.0 and

in 1970, it was 4.6. The difference in these death rates was least in 1950 at 3.6.

Discussion. Specific biological variables, although requisites, do not "cause" death in the sense that they are the immediate antecedents of death behavior. Rather, the effects of biology may be viewed as mediated through symbols-- meanings and definitions. In other words, biological variables may affect death behavior through the conditions they present to the individual but the behavioral response of death at the individual level, is to the meanings of the biology, not the biology per se.

Clearly, the religious experience of Mormons generally endorses meanings of death that are distinctive in comparison with other groups. Coupled with these distinctive death meanings is the health-related position of the L.D.S. Church as illustrated in their "Word of Wisdom". Examination of Mormon versus U.S. and Utah death rates indicates that although some SES and age[5] biases may be operating, Mormons are somewhat responsive to their religious health-and death-related definitions. The path by which health-related definitions lead to dying is somewhat obvious. Not so apparent however is the path by which religious definitions lead to dying behavior. Research is called for. Research by Robert Gardner (10) involving students at a Seventh-Day Adventist college found that the SDA and the LDS patterns of beliefs are fairly alike. There is reason to believe that the death rates may also be somewhat comparable. Comparisons of the two groups may provide insight into the variable patterns involved.

On the other hand, in their death behavior, Mormons have also shown sensitivity towards the larger society in which they exist. The similarities in death behavior patterns throughout fifty years suggest that non-Mormon audience(s) and situation(s) may serve as reference points for Mormons in their death behavior. Mormons are responsive to both their church and their society. How the two "messages" or inputs are received and synthesized to produce the patterns identified in the research remains to be studied. Little is known about how death meanings influence the process of biological death. The death-related data here presented may also be seen as one aspect of a larger "revolution" in our interpretations of human behavior in general in which we are becoming increasingly aware of the social and the symbolic components of human behavior. Explanations of such behavior which focus primarily upon biological factors are being found to be inadequate to explain the available research findings.

In conclusion, Mormon death behavior may be interpreted as a form of social behavior in response to health-and death-related symbols of their church, relative to the audience(s) and situation(s) of the larger culture. Examination of the fuller meanings of Mormon health-and death-related definitions as well as other death-related phenomena is needed in order to more clearly understand dying as a form of social behavior.

REFERENCES

1. Pearson, K. The Chances of Death, New York: Edward Arnold Publisher, 1897.

2. Vernon, G. M. Sociology of Death, New York: Ronald Press, 1970.

3. Coleman, P. "Medical Technology and Death-Related Attitudes" in Death Meanings ed. G. Vernon, Salt Lake City: Association for the Study of Religion, 1973:60-74.

4. Kalish, R. "Dividing the Invisible," Social Science and Medicine, 1968 2:249-259.

5. Nyberg, K. L. The Learning of Death, Choosing to Die, presented at the Rocky Mountain Social Science Association, Laramie, Wyoming, 1973.

6. Vernon, G.M. Human Interaction, 2nd ed., New York: Ronald Press, 1972.

7. Spicer, J.C. and S.O. Gustavus, "Mormon Fertility Through Half a Century: A Test of the Americanization Hypothesis," Social Biology, 1974,21:70-76.

8. Statistical Abstracts of the United States, U.S. Gov't.Documents, 1922-1972.

9. Vernon, G.M. "Comparative Mormon Attitudes Toward Death" in Death Meanings. ed. G.Vernon, Salt Lake City: Association for the Study of Religion, 1973: 75-80.

10. Gardner, R., "Comparative Seventh-Day Adventist Pre-medical and Nursing Students Attitudes Toward Death," unpublished paper, University of Utah, 1973.

FOOTNOTES

*Thanks are given to J. Grant Ensign of the Archival Section of the Historical Department of the Church of Jesus Christ of Latter-Day Saints for his assistance in compiling the data used in this research.

1. Biological occurrence--all cells are dead; clinical occurrence--organs of the body no longer function as a unit; psychological occurrence--self-awareness is irreversibly lost; social occurrence--roles or functions have ceased; and sociological occurrence--rejection and cut off from community.

2. The pronatalist position of the Church of Jesus Christ of Latter-Day Saints is documented by Spicer and Gustavus (7).

3. In 1970, Hawaii had a death rate of 5.5 per 1,000 and Alaska had a death rate of 4.8 per 1,000. Areas having the highest death rate in the United States were Washington, D.C., Virginia, and Missouri with 13.9, 11.6, and 11.3 per 1,000 respectively (8).

4. Death rates by the ten leading causes of death are not reported in a standardized fashion by states before 1942 in Statistical Abstracts.

5. Mormon age-specific death rates are not available from the Church's Archival Section.

CHAPTER 6

COMPARATIVE SEVENTH-DAY ADVENTIST PRE-MEDICAL
AND NURSING STUDENT ATTITUDES TOWARD DEATH

Robert W. Gardner

The theme of death has been explored by philosophers, theologians, poets, and writers throughout man's history. Despite this fact and considering that death is a phenomenon of wide and deep personal significance, knowledge of how man relates to death is meager. Man seems to have placed a taboo on thoughts and discussion about death. Perhaps this signifies an attempt to avoid or deny its existence. There is evidence that under the influence of technological, cultural, and social changes the silence is being broken. Increasing attention is being directed to problems concerned with man's relationship to death. Social scientists, who seemingly have also fallen prey to the taboo, are beginning to accumulate research findings which are directed at this area of social phenomena.

Numerous perspectives have contributed to the sociology of death; the symbolic interaction viewpoint is the most influential of these. A major strength of this position is that it stresses that dying, like living, is a matter of definition. Vernon (1970) has pointed out that death-related behavior is in response to symbols relative to the audience and the situation. The fact that death is socially defined means that information about death as a social phenomenon can be gained only by observing human behavior, both verbal and nonverbal. It also means that attitudes toward death are various and open to test.

Empirical studies of the individual's relationship to death have been comparatively few and recent. Attempts are now being made to study individual feelings and attitudes about the meaning of death. Using various techniques, sociologists are exploring the complex patterns of individual responses to death. Reactions are being obtained from various segments of the population. Certain characteristics of the individual (age, sex, religiousity, religious affiliation, education, and health) have been evaluated as affecting the meaning of death. The literature on death and the individual as a social process, rather than solely a biological one, is gradually developing.

Two social institutions, which have been the focus of several of the studies mentioned above, are closely involved with the process of dying and death. They are religion and medicine. Research done by Reily (1970) as part of a continuing program by the Equitable Life Assurance Society has pointed out that the public has a high regard for clergymen and physicians as advisers or counselors in dealing with death. Vernon (1970) has pointed out that humans often make supernatural explanations of death, and dealing with questions of what happens after death has led men to give death a religious interpretation.

Recent developments in medical science have lowered mortality rates and increased life expectancy; the doctor is often seen as having nearly supernatural control over life and death. A large spectrum of medically-trained personnel are involved in the dying process as a result of the increased percentage of deaths which occur in hospitals or other medically-oriented institutions. The close affiliation of both religion and medicine to death is unquestionable, yet they are rarely combined in research on death. Studies on the medical area often overlook, ignore, or purposefully sidestep religious relationships.

The purpose of my research is to contribute to the two areas of religion and medicine by focusing on attitudes of Seventh-day Adventist pre-medical and nursing students toward death. My study is a small replication of a larger study of college age students in the United States done by Glenn Vernon (1968). The results are compared with those found by Vernon in two areas: religious affiliation--Seventh-day Adventist attitudes will be compared with those of eleven other religious groups; and medical orientation--the attitudes of pre-medical and nursing students will be compared to the Vernon sample on medically-oriented items.

Seventh-day Adventists have been almost totally neglected in social research. Like many other smaller groups, Seventh-day Adventists are usually placed in a catch-all category and are ignored in any comparisons. Part of the "catch-all" problem results from studies done at public universities where such a small percentage of Adventists attend that the few respondents would not warrant a separate category. Therefore, since most Adventist students attend denominational colleges, this sample was taken from students at a Seventh-day Adventist institution.

The Vernon study did not include a division of students by college major or intended profession. Because of the close involvement that medical personnel have with death and dying situations, I chose students who are preparing for a medical career. Seventh-day Adventists have a higher proportion of members entering the medical professions than is found in the general population. (Sargent, 1962). It is hypothesized that the medically-oriented major will have an effect on the response to certain items which deal with medical situations. However, it is not the purpose of this research to ascertain whether Seventh-day Adventist membership or college training have the more important effect.

The results of this study are not representative of the Seventh-day Adventist Church or pre-medical and nursing students. They should be taken as suggesting some possible relationships between variables and should be used with caution. The comparisons are made with research which used the same questionnaire so that the fine points of meaning could be kept constant. Considering the lack of findings dealing with the Seventh-day Adventist Church and the pre-medical and nursing categories, analyses of the findings are informative for at least these two groupings.

RESEARCH PROJECT

The data was collected by utilizing the same questionnaire used by Vernon (1968). The 44-item questionnaire asks both open and close-ended questions on a wide variety of points dealing with attitudes toward death, including personal, religious, medical, ethical, and other areas. A list of all pre-medical and nursing students in attendance at Walla Walla College, a Seventh-day Adventist liberal arts college, was obtained from the registrar. A systematic random sample was chosen from each group resulting in 27 pre-meds and 15 nursing students. The questionnaire was distributed by dormitory assistants to the various students. Some of the students were not able to be contacted, and the return resulted in 21 pre-meds and 13 nurses, which is a return of 81%. The answers were hand-tabulated and percentage distributions were made for each item. The response patterns can be seen in Appendix A.

RESEARCH FINDINGS

Religious Affiliation

In the small reader on death, Death Meanings, Vernon discusses Mormon attitudes toward death in comparison with other religious groups. He points out that the Mormons are distinctive in their responses concerning both religious and non-religious oriented dimensions of death. The Seventh-day Adventist data was gathered separately and with different sampling techniques from the Vernon data. However, the same questionnaire was used which reduced the chance of meaning variation in questions and responses. The SDA data should not be considered as a part of the larger Vernon sample, but the comparisons made are interesting nevertheless, and analyses may be fruitful.

The following data is a reproduction of the report in Death Meanings (1973: 76,77) with the SDA percentages inserted in the proper rank order. There are twelve religious groups ranked from high to low percentage according to answers in a given way. The relative rank of the SDA respondents can be seen in comparison to the other groups.

Religiously Oriented Dimensions

The wording of the question as it appeared on the questionnaire is used.

1. Is it your personal belief that there will be a future existence of some kind after death? Percent answering "yes": Mormon 92.0, SDA 91.0, Catholic 77.5, Baptist 70.7, Lutheran 69.0, Jewish 65.3, Methodist 61.0, Episcopalian 52.1, Congregational 49.5, "Protestant" 48.8, Presbyterian 48.6, and Independent 25.9.

2. Do you have a strong wish to live after death? Percent answering "yes": Mormon 88.4, SDA 88.0, Lutheran 63.8, Catholic 61.1, Baptist 59.7, Jewish 52.7, Methodist 50.2, Presbyterian 45.7, "Protestant" 44.2, Congregational 43.8, Episcopalian 37.0, and Independent 20.0.

3. Do you anticipate reunion with your loved ones in an afterlife? Percent answering "yes": SDA 94.0, Mormon 90.2, Catholic 52.8, Baptist 52.5, Lutheran 51.7, Presbyterian 42.9, Methodist 40.9, "Protestant" 34.9, Jewish 34.7, Congregational 34.1, Episcopalian 28.8, and Independent 16.5.

4. Do you feel that religious observances by the living can somehow benefit the state of those already dead? Percent answering "yes": Mormon 67.6, Catholic 65.7, Jewish 38.0, "Protestant" 18.6, Episcopalian 13.7, Baptist 13.3, Methodist 11.9, Independent 11.8, Presbyterian 8.6, Lutheran 8.6, Congregational 7.2, and SDA 0.0.

5. Have your religious experiences in general served to increase or decrease fear toward your own death? Percent answering "Decrease fear": SDA 88.0, Mormon 85.8, Lutheran 63.8, Jewish 60.7, Presbyterian 60.0, Methodist 59.5, Episcopalian 58.9, Catholic 57.1, Baptist 56.9, "Prostent" 55.8, Congregational 51.9, and Independent 20.0.

6. Please indicate which of the following best expresses your concept of immortality: Biological, social, work accomplishments, transcendental, don't believe in immortality. Percent answering "Transcendental": Mormon 68.7, Lutheran 65.6, Catholic 61.2, SDA 59.0, Baptist 53.0, Methodist 39.0, Jewish 35.3, Presbyterian 34.3, "Protestant" 27.9, Episcopalian 27.4, Congregational 26.9, and Independent 8.2.

7. If you knew positively that there was no life after death in store for you, do you think that your manner of living in the present would be changed? Percent answering "Considerable change" and "Extensive change": Mormon 46.6, Catholic 30.6, SDA 29.0, Jewish 22.0, Episcopalian 21.9, Baptist 21.0, Lutheran 19.0, Methodist 17.1, "Protestant" 16.3, Congregational 12.5, Independent 9.4, and Presbyterian 8.6.

8. Does the question of a future life worry you considerably? Percent answering "no": Presbyterian 85.7, SDA 82.0, Mormon 80.7, Congregational 78.4, Independent 75.3, Methodist 74.0, Episcopalian 74.0, "Protestant" 69.8, Lutheran 63.8, Catholic 62.7, Jewish 62.0, and Baptist 59.7.

9. Would you prefer to know about the future life positively or would you prefer to have it left a matter of faith belief? Percent answering "know positively": Independent 51.8, Mormon 51.3, Catholic 43.8, Presbyterian 37.1, Jewish 36.0, Lutheran 34.5, Methodist 32.7, Congregational 31.7, Baptist 31.5, "Protestant" 27.9, SDA 24.0, and Episcopalian 23.3.

The most significant factor about the SDA distribution was that out of the nine religious items, the SDA respondents were either one of the two highest or two lowest in seven out of the nine categories. Although the SDA pattern is certainly different from any other single religious group, they do not distinguish themselves from all the groups in any distinct way. The Mormon pattern which Vernon discusses is quite comparable to the SDA responses on several items. The attitudes of SDA's, like Mormons, could be described as being a transcendental belief in an other-worldly life where they could reunite with loved ones who have died. They do not fear death appreciably and find that faith is a strong proof for their after life beliefs. They also feel that there is reward in their present life for living according to their religious beliefs. The most distinctly different SDA response was concerning the capability of the living to affect the state of the dead. The zero response to that question indicates a different interpretation of death.

The fact that the SDA responses closely parallel the Mormon ones, on six of nine items, suggests that Vernon's conclusion of a distinctive interpretation and experience of death for the Mormons is questionable. After inserting the data on SDA's, the only distinctive response by Mormons was on item seven dealing with the change in lifestyle if there were no life after death. That particular response might be indicative of a strong social control element in the "Mormon experience."

Although with the SDA data Mormons are no longer singularly distinctive on a number of items, SDA's and Mormons together are distinctive from the other groups. These items deal with beliefs of an afterlife and reunion with loved ones. The explanation of this difference may not lie so much in a "Mormon experience" as in a certain Biblical belief or fundamentalist position.

Furthermore, the intellectual dimension of religiousity discussed by Glock and Stark (1965) might be a factor. Those who intellectually know their church's doctrine about death may be distinct from those who don't. The majority of Mormon and SDA respondents were students at their respective denominational colleges and might be representative of a more "intellectual" group concerning their church doctrines. Certainly the information from this survey cannot provide a full and adequate explanation of the differences and similarities found among Seventh-day Adventists and other religious groups, in particular the Mormons. However, the evidence does seem to indicate that the position that the Mormons have a "distinctive interpretation and experience of death" should be questioned, for on many points they share it with SDA's.

Non-Religiously Oriented Dimensions

Vernon also stated that the Mormons as a group were also distinctive in their answers concerning the non-religiously oriented items on death. Analysis of the SDA responses on the non-religious items brings this statement into question also.

1. How frequently do you think of your own death? Percent answering "very rarely" and "rarely": Mormon 61.1, SDA 59.0, Presbyterian 48.5, Jewish 47.3, Independent 47.0, Episcopalian 46.6, Lutheran 44.9, Methodist 44.2, Congregational 44.2, "Protestant" 44.2, Baptist 37.0, and Catholic 39.7.

2. Do you approve of cremation for others? Percent answering "no":
Jewish 51.3, Mormon 45.1, Catholic 28.3, Baptist 21.0, Lutheran 19.0,
"Protestant" 14.0, SDA 12.0, Methodist 11.9, Congregational 10.1, Independ-
ent 9.4, Presbyterian 8.6, and Episcopalian 6.8.

3. Do you approve of cremation for yourself? Percent answering "no":
Jewish 84.0, Mormon 78.5, Catholic 60.9, Baptist 51.9, Lutheran 50.0,
Methodist 43.5, Presbyterian 40.0, "Protestant" 32.6, Congregational 30.8,
Episcopalian 23.3, Independent 17.6, and SDA 6.0.

4. Childhood questions about death were generally answered
adequately. Percent answering "yes": SDA 88.0, Mormon 81.5, Episcopalian
72.6, Congregational 71.6, Baptist 71.3, Catholic 70.8, Presbyterian 65.7,
Lutheran 65.5, Methodist 62.5, "Protestant" 60.5, Jewish 54.7, and
Independent 47.1.

5. It has been suggest that a unit of study on the "mental hygiene
of grief" be developed and taught in our schools, much the same way that
physical hygiene is taught. What do you think of this idea? Percent
answering "I agree": SDA 35.0, "Protestant" 32.6, Mormon 32.0, Presbyterian 31.4, Independent 30.6, Baptist 26.5, Congregational 25.5,
Methodist 24.9, Catholic 23.2, Episcopalian 20.5, Jewish 19.3, and Lutheran 10.3.

6. Do you feel that you could currently adequately face the death
of a loved one? Percent answering "yes": SDA 68.0, Mormon 62.2, Independent 50.6, "Protestant" 48.8, Congregational 45.2, Catholic 43.6,
Methodist 42.0, Episcopalian 39.7, Lutheran 36.2, Baptist 35.9, Presbyterian 34.3, and Jewish 29.3.

7. Have you ever seriously discussed the subject of death--not in
reference to a specific incident or disaster, but as a general concept
which applies universally to all human beings? Percent answering "yes":
Mormon 83.6, SDA 76.0, Episcopalian 74.0, Presbyterian 71.4, Jewish 69.3,
Congregational 69.2, Catholic 68.9, Independent 63.5, Baptist 61.9,
Lutheran 60.3, Methodist 58.0, and "Protestant" 53.5.

On five of seven of the items SDA responses and Mormon responses were
similar. Vernon's description of the Mormon pattern on items which were
not religious in nature could be used to describe the SDA pattern except
for one point, cremation.

> "They . . . indicate that their childhood questions were
> answered adequately, that they have discussed death as an
> abstract subject, approve of school study of the mental
> hygiene of grief, but rarely think of their own death . . .
> and believe that they could adequately face the death of a
> loved one." (Vernon, 1973: 80)

The SDA respondents favored cremation for themselves and others while
the Mormons largely rejected it. Although SDA's approve of it less for
others than for themselves, they approve of it for themselves far more than
any other group.

50

The responses of SDA's on the non-religious items were more likely to be less extreme than they were on the religious items. However; they were either one of the first two or last two on six of the seven items. Perhaps there is a distinctiveness between religious groups on attitudes of death, but it apparently is not restricted to SDA's or Mormons.

Medical Orientation

The respondents to this survey are not only SDA's but students with a medical orientation, i.e. pre-medical and nursing students. Because they are students, it is likely that their actual medical experience is limited, yet they all would have a medical profession as a relevant reference group. The results of the two groups, pre-medical and nursing, are not appreciably different, so their results are analyzed as a medically-oriented college group and not as two separate groups. Their responses will not be compared with other SDA non-medically oriented students but with the total sample responses found by Vernon in his study. The results in this instance should be interpreted as suggestive of the medically-oriented group, but certainly not representative. The religious factor in this case is of no concern, although it may be an important factor. The Vernon figures are of a mixed sampling of students and others with various academic and professional orientation. Again the results are only suggestive of differences resulting from the medically-oriented relevant reference group.

1. It has been suggested that a unit of study on the "mental hygiene of grief" be developed and taught in schools, much the same way that physical hygiene is taught. What do you think of this idea?

MED	VERNON	
35.0	26.5	I agree that this should be done.
18.0	24.6	I disagree. Since grief is such a personal experience, each must handle it in his or her own way.
41.0	41.3	I don't feel I've considered this subject sufficiently to express an opinion concerning it.

2. How many times have you actually seen a dead body before it was prepared by the mortician?

MED	VERNON	
38.0	14.6	Three or more

3. Would you prefer to know about the future life positively (scientifically), or would you prefer to have it left a matter of faith or belief?

MED	VERNON	
24.0	39.6	Know positively (scientifically)
76.0	58.5	Left to faith or belief

51

4. Do you approve of mercy killing in cases of extreme suffering?

MED	VERNON	
18.0	40.0	No
15.0	17.2	Yes
53.0	22.7	Yes, in some cases
9.0	16.4	Yes, but only if the lethal agent is self-administered or requested by the patient

5. Do you feel that if an individual is dying and is beyond any available medical aid that it is more desirable to remove the person to a hospital or other institution, rather than have him remain at home?

MED	VERNON	
26.0	33.8	Yes, this is the best course for all concerned
35.0	28.6	No, death should be at home, if at all possible
38.2	35.2	Undecided

6. If you contracted a fatal illness, do you feel you would want to be told that you would most likely die?

MED	VERNON	
91.0	71.2	Yes
6.0	15.3	No
3.0	11.7	Undecided

An analysis of the above items points out a number of interesting things. Medically-oriented students favor a class in the "mental hygiene of grief" more than a general group of students. This reaction may be related to their orientation towards school and knowledge being received in the classroom. Like the general group, they didn't feel that they had considered the subject enough. They had come in contact with dead bodies quite frequently which may be related to actual medical experiences in school or to previous experiences which may have led them to choose the medical profession. A surprising number of them preferred to leave the question of life after death to faith and religion. They apparently view this factor as religious rather than scientific concern. This indicates that the religious experiences of this medically-oriented group may have a strong effect on their views toward death. Whether this effect carries on after further medical training and practice would be an interesting area of further research.

Vernon reported that the majority of his respondents approved of mercy killing under certain circumstances. He further asserted that "American society appears to be changing in the direction of greater approval." (Vernon, 1973:30). The findings of my study would support this position, because even a larger majority of the medically-oriented respondents approved of it than those from Vernon's general group. Medical personnel as a group have typically opposed mercy killing, giving preference to preservation of life at all costs; however, as noted by Dr. Neumann in a class lecture, the trend towards favoring mercy killing may be increasing among young physicians. It is likely that the trend will continue if pre-medical and nursing students highly favor such an action.

Little difference between groups is noted on the item concerning location of dying and death. However, it may be significant that a medically-oriented group responded that home and not the hospital is the best place, which is opposite from the general group response.

The last item concerning knowledge of a fatal illness may be the most significant of all. Feifel (1963:12) reported from his study that medically trained persons do not, and felt that they should not, discuss fatal illness with their patients. He also suggests that the dying patient would like to have his doctor discuss his condition with him. Other studies have found similar results, i.e. Kasper and Kalish. In another study Feifel found that the physician himself would like to know if he had contracted a fatal illness; however, he was still reluctant to report such a condition to his own patients. The findings in this survey certainly bear out Feifel's conclusion, and it appears that medical training must emphasize at some point that it is harmful for medical personnel to discuss impending death with a fatally ill person.

Clearly the medically-oriented person, whether real or in terms of a relevant reference group, reveals a distinct pattern towards death. It may be that there are distinct differences in attitudes toward death which are related not only to religion but to a person's academic or professional orientation. It has been suggested by some limited evidence that one of the factors involved in a person choosing a medically-oriented career is the fear of death (Vernon, 1970:202). The evidence found in this survey certainly would not support such a position. The medically-oriented respondents did not show a higher fear of death than the general group. If fear of death is a motivating factor, it is not found among the SDA medically-oriented group. These findings are suggestive that the fear of death, illustrated by hesitancy to discuss death with a terminally ill patient, may result from medical training, not from some pre-existing fear that motivated the person into the field.

SDA medically-oriented respondents may have a lower fear of death than other medical professionals, which would definitely be related to their religion and perhaps their medical training in parochial schools. The findings are also suggestive that the SDA medically-oriented person has a distinctive interpretation which may result in his meeting death situations with less fear and fewer personal problems than other groups. However, the findings are only suggestive and are not representative of the SDA medical category. It is recommended that the religious orientation of medical personnel be taken into account on future research in this area.

CONCLUSION

Increasing attention is being given to man's relationship to dying and death by social scientists. This study, a small replication of an earlier study by Vernon (1968), is a contribution to this growing body of literature.

By utilizing the Vernon questionnaire, Seventh-day Adventist pre-medical and nursing students' attitudes toward death were collected, compiled, and analyzed. The results were compared with Vernon's findings in two areas: SDA attitudes compared to thirteen other religious groups, and pre-medical and nursing student responses to medically-oriented items.

Vernon's conclusion that Mormons have a distinct view of death was found to be questionable on all items compared. SDA's were most distinctive on their views toward cremation and the ability of the living to affect the condition of the dead.

The medically-oriented respondents revealed a distinct pattern toward death. Influential was the finding that this group did not exhibit as much fear toward death as the general group. They also supported the conclusion that Americans are increasing their approval of mercy killing under certain circumstances.

This small study suggests that future research on death and dying among medically-oriented persons should be aware of the strength and pervasiveness of the religious factor. More research is needed to determine the effect of academic, pre-professional, and professional training on a person's view of death.

The time, way, and manner in which medical training effects an individual's view of death is also needed. It would also be interesting to determine which has the greater effect on death-related behavior--religious definitions or medical definitions of death for the medically-oriented person. Obviously there is a great deal of much needed research in the area.

This study has also added to the sociological knowledge about Seventh-day Adventists who have long been ignored by the social researcher for various reasons. This paper is seen as contributing to the development of a Sociology of Seventh-day Adventists.

BIBLIOGRAPHY

Brim, Orville G., Jr., Howard E. Freeman, Sol Levine, and Norman A. Scotch, ed. The Dying Patient. Russel Sage Foundation, New York, 1970.

Feifel, Herman. "Death," in Taboo Topics, ed. Norman L. Farberow. Atherton Press, New York, 1963.

Glock, Charles Y. Religion and Society in Tension. Rand McNally, Chicago, 1965.

Quint, Jeanne C. The Nurse and the Dying Patient. Macmillan Company, New York, 1967.

Reiley, John W. "Death: death and bereavement," in International Encyclopedia of the Social Sciences (1968), 19-26.

Scott, Frances G., ed. Confrontations of Death. Continuing Education Publications, Corvallis, Oregon, 1971.

Vernon, Glenn. "A Study of Attitudes Toward Death." (Unpublished, analysis in process.)

_____. Death Meanings. Association for the Study of Religion, Salt Lake City, Utah, 1973.

_____. Sociology of Death. Ronald Press Company, New York, 1970.

CHAPTER 7

DISGUISED THEOLOGIANS: THE ANTI-IMMORTALISTS*

Glenn M. Vernon
University of Utah

Introduction

In the area of death-related behavior there are widespread beliefs or interpretations incorporating some version of the premise that biological death is not the end of the individual, but rather the beginning of some different type of existence. Those accepting such beliefs have been identified as "immortalists." This is the label which will be used here. An alternate descriptive label is that they are "denying death." This is the case of the book by Ernest Becker which be will be analyzing, titled "The Denial of Death." Actually the anti-immortalists do not deny the existence of biological death, but rather of any type of existence beyond death. They accept the finality of biological death.

Those who accept the premise that biological death is the end of the individual and thus deny the existence of any immortality, will be called "anti-immortalists." To them death is the end of the individual. For them there is nothing of the individual which continues, as an individual, after death.

The anti-immortalists are basically developing the following argument:
1. Biological death is a universal phenomenon.
2. Biological death is the end of the individual--there is nothing beyond biological death.
3. Those who believe in immortality or who accept the premise that there is something beyond death, are accepting false beliefs. To do so is unhealthy or wrong.
4. Some, such as Becker, develop the premise that a "healthy" adjustment requires unqualified acceptance of the fact of there being no immortality.
5. Some such as Harrington, accept the ancient injunction of Guatama (Amore: 122) "Death conquers all, so conquer death."

In religious terms, the anti-immortalists write to call the immortalists' to repentance and to provide them with a blueprint for the road to "salvation" thru (1) death acceptence or (2) conquoring death per se.

Post-Biological-Death Condition

While decisions have obviously been reached by those using both perspectives about the post-death condition, a basic question of concern regardless of what the conclusion is, is how does one reach conclusions about the post-death situation.

Immortalists. There is no empirical or scientific evidence that there is some type of spiritual or non-empirical existence after death. Those immortalists who accept the conclusion that there is a life after death are utilizing a faith-type method of securing answers. It requires a leap of faith, which takes the acceptors beyond the empirical world, into the non-referented, symbolic world. Such answers transcend the empirical world.

* Paper presented at the annual meeting of the Pacific Sociological Assoc., Victoria, B. C., April 1975.

The immortalists typically present themselves as theologians or as accepting theological answers.

Anti-immortalists. How do the anti-immortalists differ in their conclusion of no afterlife from the immortalists in their conclusion of an afterlife? The content of the conclusions is obviously different but how about the method? What is not so obvious to some is that the method used in each case is identical. A faith-type method is involved. There are no conclusive empirical scientific answers one way or the other.

The anti-immortalists however frequently seem to operate from the premise or at least give the impression of doing so, that their position is one of science. "Science has proven that there is nothing beyond the grave" is their starting premise. How science has proven this is apparently rarely if ever considered, and the steps involved in such proving are not specified. They do not explain how a scientific method restricted to empirical phenomena can be used to reach decisions about non-empirical phenomena.

Actually one has to accept the anti-immortalist premise upon faith not upon empirical evidence. However, in contrast with the immortalists the anti-immortalists generally deny their theological stance, and apparently fail to recognize that if the immortalists are in effect condemned by their method, the anti-immortalists are equally condemning themselves. The anti-immortalists seem to be doing their religion in the name of the non-religion or in the name of science.

As is frequently true of those who utilize a theological approach the anti-immortalists seek to validate or legitimate their particular beliefs (fears, definitions) by figuratively or symbolically locating their phenomenon of concern in the biology of the person, or in a creating power behind the biology--i.e. the gods.

In doing so they place these causes of behavior outside the realm of scientific proof. Acceptance of them requires some faith-type method. In their effort to secure converts the anti-immortalists attempt to use many of the most effective conversion methods available. One such technic is to define the problem so that nothing can be done about it except thru util-ization of the services of the expert--i.e. the one making the claim. In this category, for instance, is the psychoanalyst who maintains that the only way one can learn about his "real self" is to go thru psychoanalysis, and thus have the expert tell him what he couldn't find out for himself. The only way one can find out about his real beliefs is to have the expert discover the beliefs for him.

The Anti-Immortalist Perspective

The last ten years or so has seen a remarkable increase in societal concern with death-related behavior. As a part of this "movement" a few prominent anti-immortalists have stepped forward to present their writing supporting the anti-immoralists position. Since they have made the effort to present their beliefs in writing they seem to be seeking for converts to their position. It does not seem to be inappropriate to use Hoffer's label of "true believers" to identify them.

This paper is not written to even suggest that the anti-immortalists are wrong in their conclusions. The major purpose is to suggest that they be classified where they belong, as religionists who are presenting as forcefully as they can, a religious perspective to which they apparently have a strong personal commitment. To the extent that religious conclusions are presented as being scientific in nature, it appears that distorted evidence has been introduced and used in the effort to achieve their desired social action goal. Distortion of this type has frequently been utilized by those with a religious message which they attempt to present with great zeal. If this is being done, the readers should know of it.

An analysis of the theological grounds upon which the anti-immortalist position is developed will now be presented. We will focus primarily upon the writings of Alan Harrington and Ernest Becker.

Harrington

Harrington's basic premise is that there is no life after death and thus the only immortality possible is for humans themselves to conquer death per se. He suggests, for instance (p. 125) that "The species must solve the problem of death very soon, blow itself up, or blow its mind." The time has come, he says, for humans to get rid of the "intimidating gods" in their own heads. It is time for humans to grow up, out of a cosmic inferiority complex (no more "dust thou art, and to dust thou shalt return...") bring the disgussed desire into the open, and go after what they really want, the only state of being they will settle for, which is divinity. (p. 26)

Beliefs in immortality are discredited by use of terms like "elaborate pretense," "disguised drive," "intimidating gods in his own head," and statements such as "an intolerable recognition only now emerging to general consciousness; with protective myths and orthodoxies having been stripped away, not merely the knowledge but the gut-realization that the void is waiting for everybody and that each of us is going to vanish into it."

Justification for his anti-immortalist position rests upon "evidence" such as the statement that "since the beginning of recorded time man has engaged in a disguised drive to make himself immortal and devine." This overriding motive is presented as accounting for much of human action, and is now driving man toward his evolutionary crisis. "The time has come to turn into gods or perish." (p. 29)

Harrington further says that those who indicate that they welcome death or are not afraid of death maintain what he calls an "elaborate pretense" of not wanting to survive. Just how he knows that such is an elaborate pretense and that his anti-immortalist position is not the "elaborate pretense" is, of course, not specified.

Harrington extensively utilizes authority as his proof. He makes authoritative statements on his own. He, however, never gets around to telling us the source of his "revelation" or inspiration. One wonders, without ever finding out in his book, just how he knows the truths he proclaims.

He also follows the pattern of the immortalists by holding out a Utopia which is going to be just great for everyone. He, however, never really looks squarely at any of the possible consequences of living in such a Utopian state. Maybe before anyone uncritically accepts the premise that such an existence (sans death) would be very desirable they ought to make sure they understand just what they would be letting themselves in for. They may then conclude that a death is a gift each of us gives to generations as yet unborn. Some relevant questions concerning such a deathless society are as follows:

1. What about aging? Would conquering death scientifically mean that individuals would continue to age but just not die? If aging could be arrested, would this be accomplished at say age 21, and thus preserve the individuals at that age forever, or would it be only accomplished when terminal illness threatened death?

2. Would existing biological defects be perpetuated for eternity? Would our medical (biological) advances merely extend life or would there also be some restorative components?

3. If there were no death, there would be no capital punishment. Threatening to take one's life would be meaningless. What would be the consequences as far as criminal behavior is concerned?

4. Would non-death be manditory for everyone, or only for those who, according to some set of rules, qualified for it?

5. Would maintaining a non-death status require constant "medication" or whatever was involved? If constant attention of some kind was required would the result be worth the price?

6. Would the elimination of death eliminate war? Would there be much liklihood of going to war if no one could be killed? Would we possibly continue warring but preserve the maimed injured, disfigured individuals eternally?

7. Would moral standards be permanent and unchanging or would society constantly change them?

8. What would happen to established marriage patterns. Would most married couples willing spend eternity with their current spouse?

9. If aging continued what would happen to sexual satisfaction?

10. What would happen to the medical profession. Would we need more or less (or any) physicians? Would it be possible to cure all diseases, or would diseases linger on in an unresolved stage while the individual continued to "live."

11. Would physicians be needed to maintain the non-death condition? Would physicians have to continue their treatments forever?

12. What would a no-death society do about births?

13. How about occupations? Jobs would never be vacated by death. Would more and more positions be needed for a growing population assuming that there would be births? Would people ever retire permanently? If so, what would they do? Would there possibly be an established pattern of job rotation in which I would be a lawyer for 100 years, a carpenter for the next 100 years, a grocery man for the next, and etc.?

14. If there are no built-in limits would anything be valued? If anything could eventually be achieved by everyone, would there be much value associated with anything?

15. Would eating continue to be pleasurable?

16. Would pain be intensified and eternally prolonged?

17. Would non-death be restricted to humans or expanded to other animals. if so what would happen to diets which include meat?

18. Would we require a completely controlled society?
19. What would happen to recreation and arts?
20. Do we assume that physical health would somehow automatically be associated with or result in mental health. Would we want to maintain physical health if there was nothing we could do about poor mental health. Would living forever add to mental health or mental illness? Would everyone need a personal psychiatrist? And then what would the psychiatrists do?

Religion. In his Utopia there is apparrently no need for religion, since religion is seen as being involved in the perpetuation of beliefs that there is a life after death. Some students who considered the question of whether there would be a need for religion in such a death-less existence, concluded that indeed there would be a great need for religion. The basic message of the religion they envisioned was that members of the society should hold fast to the faith, believing that if they just lived worthy of it, there would in truth in the future be a death for them. Worthy believers would be entitled to a death.

Ernest Becker

Becker's "The Denial of Death" concerns much more than just death-related behavior. It presents a comprehensive interpretation of human behavior which incorporated premises about death beliefs, as one part thereof. The comments made here are only in an indirect way related to the total model he presents. We focus upon just the one component thereof.

The title of the book is misleading. It is not concerned with denial of death, but with a denial of immortality or some post-death existence. Belief in immortality denies the finality of death. Becker, however, denies immortality and hence will be labeled "anti-immortalist."

He develops the premise that the human life time is spent with the "fear of death haunting even his most sun-filled days" (jacket). This fear of death which is seen as being innate and hence universal to humans, is conceived of as the major source of human activity. Stemming from this universal fear of death, is the human effort to transcend death in culturally standardized ways--thru heroics, narcissim, charisma, religion and neurosis.

For our analysis two pertinent questions are (1) how do we know that the fear exists universally? and (2) if it is a universal phenomenon, how do we know what the consequences of this universality are?

Unversal Fear. From the evidence in the book we have to conclude that the universality of this fear of death is something which is posited not proven. It is not supported by empirical research. This, of course, does not prove its non-existence.

Becker, however, indicated that once we understand that the struggle against death is at the very heart of human life, the way is left open for a truly revolutionary cooperation between religion and science. Whether one ends up with a "cooperation" between religion and science is doubtful. As has been suggested, one ends up doing his anti-immortalist religion in the name of science. An anti-immortalist position is accepted upon faith, not scientific evidence.

60

If the struggle against death is really at the very heart of human life, as Becker suggests, or if it is at the heart of all human life, it is a common element in tremendously diverse types of behavior and beliefs. From a research perspective, with a goal of predicting future behavior, the predictive or explanatory power of a "universal fear of death" is next to nil. You can't in fact, explain much of anything from knowledge about a variable which is present in all types of behavior. There are no non-variable types of behavior with which to make comparisons. Everything that is done is seen as being related to the universal factor.

What Becker does is present another of the one-factor determinisms or one-factor analyses which ignores the complexity of human interaction, and the human ability to place literally anything at the center or the core of evaluations around which living is oriented.

The same analysis is applicable to Harrington's statement (p. 15) that "the fact of death alone, all by itself, may be what is at the core of the human neurosis." (emphasis added)

Becker relates his "fear of death component" to what he calls the existential delemma, or the fact that man has both a biological body and the ability to symbolically transcend that biological base. Man, he says, has a symbolic self. He is a creature with a name, and a life history. He is a creator with a mind that soars out to speculate about atoms and infinity, who can place himself imaginatively at a point in space and contemplate bemusedly his own planet. This immense expansion, this dexterity, this ethereality, this self-consciousness gives to man literally the status of a small god in nature.(p. 26)

Man's symbols provide freedom, his body imposes a predetermined fate. From Becker's perspective the body is an inferior, phenomenon. He discusses biology in terms of "anality" rather than "brainality." He emphasized that the king always is sitting on "shit" (to use his wording) implying that this is symbolic of the whole body. Actually "the king" isn't so sitting. The "king" sits on a throne. The king includes many biological components including the biological mechansims required to create and respond to symbols. Becker's perception is highly selective. He confuses internal with individual-level phenomenon. He makes an initial decision that the body is bad and then structures his analysis to harmonize with that evaluation. Death then is a negative factor since it is something which happens to the body, or at the body level. The god-like qualities of symboling are, however, as much related to the body as is any anal activity.

What we have in his analysis is an illustration of stacking the "psychoanalytic cards" to arrive at a pre-determined conclusion. Nothing is proven except that the cards (symbols) can be so stacked.

Further, as our discussion of Harrington's proposed conquoring of death brought out, a predetermined fate of death may not be all that bad.

Universals

There is a very meaningful distinction between the biological aspects of human behavior and the symbolic aspects. These, in turn are both differentiated from the behavioral aspects. Behavior of interacting individuals involves biological beings responding to symbolic input and is thus a symbolic-biological phenomenon. If in explaining human behavior one wants to take the "universal route" there are some interesting questions such as the following which need attention.

If you assume that there is in fact something universal about death-realted behavior, where are you going to look for it --
    a. in the biology?
    b. in the symbol systems?
    c. in the interaction?

Both Harrington and Becker opt to take the biology route. That which they select to relate to man's biology is the _fear_ of death. Dying per se is a universal human condition (existential condition) about which there is no argument. Harrington does, however, posit the possible elimination of this universal biological characteristic thru manipualtion of the biology as a result of scientific advances.

Neither of the two authors ask the question of whether fear is a biological or a symbolic phenomenon. They assume it is biological. However, the best evidence today is that fear of anything is a symbolic thing. Our language which includes "fear" as a noun, however, misleads us. This is an illustration of the impact of grammar upon human behavior. Most accept unquestioningly the contrary assumption that language and the rules which govern the use thereof, have no direct influence upon perception. Language merely reflects what is "out there," or " in there." It permits us to talk in a socially accepted manner about what is empirically there, but it does not influence what we conceive of as being there.

However, if we define fear as a symbolic phenomenon, then we are faced with a question of level-jumping--i.e. jumping from the biological level to the symbolic level. The pertinent question is how can something symbolic with socially constructed arbitrary man-made meaning be provided biologically? An aspect of this phenomenon which never gets much, if any, attention is just where is the biological focus of this fear. The answer appears to be that there just is no such thing.

People learn to fear. People learn not to fear. Fearing is a symbolic process. If it is fearing death that concerns us, and if we want to posit its universality, it would be more logical then to locate the fearing within the symbolic component or possible the behavioral component of behavior. If fearing death is a universal thing, the universality is explained by some characteristic of the symbolic world, or the world of symbols. Is there something in the human use of symbols which makes everyone fear death? When we start to consider this question, we rather quickly run up against the fact that there are those who tell us that they do not fear death. What then do we do? One option is to follow Harrington's lead and label those who say they do not fear death as engaging in an "elaborate pretense." We can then maintain our orignial assumptions or our original model. We never, however, get around to knowing how to prove that the fearing and not the non-fearing is the "elaborate pretense."

If we start with the premise that it is not the meaning of anything that is biologically universal, but rather the ability to create meaning, we are off on a different journey. Neither fearing or not fearing death is universal. Either can be learned. We can then take the next step and explore differences between those who fear death and those who don't, and we can do so without the necessity of labeling one an "elaborate pretense." Each is a type of definition, which is created in interaction in a given situation.

We previously made the point that our grammar per se has an influence upon behavior, emphazing that using the concept "fear" as a noun does just that. It distorts our phenomenon of concern. Let us now look a bit further at "fear." This is a noun and thus by our rules of grammar is the name of some "person, place or thing." If we start with the assumption that it is a thing, then looking for this thing in the biology of humans is a logical next step. Further, if you can't find the "thing" empirically, it is easy to take the next step and conceptualize it as a metaphysical thing, which even if you can't find it, is a necessary component of the formula we need to round out our explanation.

If rather than using a thing-concept, "fear," we use a process concept, fearing or fearful, we have moved from a biological thing phenomenon to a behavioral or process phenomenon. Fearing behavior is something human beings do, not something they have. Further fearing behavior is related to an audience(s) and to a situation. It is social in nature. As with all behavioral phenomenon, the fearing behavior contains a symbol component. Something (death or otherwise) then is fearful when individuals real-ize the fear. They make it real by believing it. Put an individual who demonstrates fearful behavior under hypnosis and the fearful behavior is not evidenced. The same results are possible without hypnosis. Give an individual the right kinds of symbols (learning experiences) the right audience and the appropriate situation and he can be socialized to fear or not fear anything.

Neither fearing or not fearing is a universal phenomenon. Either can be socially created by those involved. You don't have to invoke any biologically provided universal to explain death fear. Attempting to do so adds nothing to our explanation. Doing so, however, may add something to the self image of the anti-immortalist in that it facilitates his acceptance of his anti-immortalist position. It permits him to maintain his religion.

Becker says that it is the human ability to symbolically transcend the empirical world and the biological body which gives one "literally the status of a small god in nature." The discussion presented here suggests that Becker did not recognize the full strength of his position. "Fearing" is a biology transcending process. To attempt to root it in biology fails to recognize the tremendous potentially of the human symboling ability.

63

It is a poor pun, but the anti-immortalists seem to be scared to death of immortality. An interesting research problem would be to see if we could get some insight into just what it is that has scared the anti-immortalists about immortality. If the model of human behavior we have just presented is an accurate one, the causes of such fearing would be found in the social experiences of the anti-immortalists not in their biology. It would be interesting to see if we could discover significant differences in the learning experiences of the immortalists and the anti-immortalists. It would also be interesting to see if there would be differences in the death-related behavior of the immortalists and the anti-immortalists. It just may be that neither belief has much of an impact upon death-related behavior.

Summary

Some believe in immortality, some do not. The anti-immortalists recognize that the immortalists reach their conclusion thru some religious method, but frequently deny that they do the same thing, thus disguising their theology by presenting it in the name of science. Neither position is scientific. Each is theological. Becker develops the premise that a healthy death-adjustment requires unqualified acceptance of anti-immortality beliefs, whereas Harrington suggests that since death conquers all, humans should (and most likely will) scientifically conquer death.

Harrington fails to ask basic questions such as those developed here about the quality of living in the society he projects. Becker suggests without providing any proof that there is a universal human fear of death from which death-related as well as living-related problems develop. The positing of such a fear, however, adds nothing to our understanding or our predictability of human behavior. Becker is victimized by his assumptions.

REFERENCES

Amore, R. C.
   1974   "The Heterodox Philosophical Systems," in Frederick H. Holck, ed.,
           Death and Eastern Thought. New York: Abingdon Press, pp. 114-193.

Becker, Ernest
   1973   The Denial of Death. New York: The Free Press.

Harrington, Alan
   1969   The Immortalist. New York: Avon Books.

CHAPTER 8

DEATH AND RELIGIOUS AFFILIATION

Some Research Findings

Glenn M. Vernon

The material presented in the following tables is taken from a larger study of the meaning of death-related behavior, which involved questionnaire answers from American college students. These respondents were secured from college campuses in various sections of the United States. They are not, however, representative of any larger group. The findings presented here are suggestive of relationships between variables but should be interpreted with caution.

The findings are presented here without analysis, primarily to make them available for research and analyses.

The material presented here involves only those respondents belonging to a religious group for which there were at least thirty five members included in the universe of study. The distribution is as follows:

Independent	85
Catholic	466
Methodist	269
Presbyterian	35
Episcopalian	73
Congregational	208
Lutheran	58
Baptist	181
Mormon	275
"Protestant"	41
Jewish	150

In the questionnaire instructions requested that the respondents identify a specific group affiliation. Despite the instructions, "Protestant" was used by some of those included. This was apparently an identification which they decided was appropriate for them.

The questionnaire asked for religious affiliation rather than religious preference.

65

1. How frequently do you think of your own death?

	Very Rarely and Rarely Percent	Occasionally Percent	Frequently Percent	Very Frequently Percent	No Answer Percent
Independent	47.0	32.9	12.9	7.1	
Catholic	39.7	43.3	14.6	1.9	.2
Methodist	44.2	42.4	11.2	1.9	.4
Presbyterian	48.5	28.6	17.1	2.9	2.9
Episcopalian	46.6	41.1	11.0	1.~	
Congregational	44.2	45.2	9.6	1.<	
Lutheran	44.9	43.1	10.3	1.7	
Baptist	37.0	40.3	16.0	6.1	.6
Mormon	61.1	29.1	7.3	2.2	.4
"Protestant"	44.2	41.9	14.0	0.0	
Total Non-Jewish	45.0	39.5	12.5	2.6	.4
Jewish	47.3	36.0	12.7	4.0	

2. If you knew positively that there was no life after death in store for you do you think that your manner of living in the present would be changed?

	Very Little Percent	Slight Change Percent	Considerable Percent	Extensive Percent	No Answer Percent
Independent	80.0	8.2	4.7	4.7	2.<
Catholic	42.1	26.4	21.2	9.4	.6
Methodist	59.1	21.9	12.3	4.8	1.9
Presbyterian	74.3	17.1	8.6	0.0	
Episcopalian	68.5	8.2	17.8	4.1	1.4
Congregational	69.2	16.8	9.1	3.4	1.4
Lutheran	58.6	20.7	13.8	5.2	1.7
Baptist	58.0	21.0	17.7	3.3	
Mormon	27.3	25.5	29.1	17.5	.4
"Protestant"	72.1	9.3	16.3	0.0	2.3
Total Non-Jewish	52.6	20.8	17.6	7.9	.9
Jewish	58.7	19.3	16.7	5.3	

66

3.Do you feel that you could currently adequately face the death of a loved one?

	Yes Percent	No Percent	Undecided Percent	No Answer Percent
Independent	50.6	22.4	27.1	
Catholic	43.6	26.4	29.6	.2
Methodist	42.0	28.6	27.9	1.5
Presbyterian	34.3	28.6	37.1	
Episcopalian	39.7	16.4	42.5	1.4
Congregational	45.2	22.1	31.7	.5
Lutheran	36.2	39.7	22.4	1.7
Baptist	35.9	33.7	29.8	
Mormon	62.2	14.9	22.5	
"Protestant"	48.8	25.6	20.9	2.3
Total Non-Jewish	46.4	23.7	29.0	.3
Jewish	29.3	35.3	34.0	.7

4. Do you have a strong wish to live after death?

	Yes Percent	No Percent	Undecided Percent	No Answer Percent
Independent	20.0	51.8	28.2	
Catholic	61.6	14.6	23.4	.4
Methodist	50.2	18.2	30.9	.4
Presbyterian	45.7	22.9	25.7	2.9
Episcopalian	37.0	19.2	39.7	4.1
Congregational	43.8	24.5	29.3	1.4
Lutheran	63.8	15.5	20.7	
Baptist	59.7	11.6	26.5	1.7
Mormon	88.4	3.6	8.0	
"Protestant"	44.2	25.6	27.9	
Total Non-Jewish	56.6	17.4	24.8	.9
Jewish	52.7	16.7	28.7	2.0

67

5. Do you approve of cremation for others?

	Yes Percent	No Percent	Undecided Percent	No Answer Percent
Independent	71.8	9.4	15.3	3.5
Catholic	51.1	28.3	19.5	.9
Methodist	63.9	11.9	23.4	.7
Presbyterian	74.3	8.6	17.1	
Episcopalian	80.8	6.8	11.0	1.4
Congregational	74.0	10.1	15.9	
Lutheran	56.9	19.0	24.1	
Baptist	50.3	21.0	26.5	1.7
Mormon	37.8	45.1	16.7	.4
"Protestant	67.4	14.0	18.6	
Total Non-Jewish	58.5	21.2	19.3	.9
Jewish	20.7	51.3	26.7	1.3

6. Do you approve of cremation for yourself?

	Yes Percent	No Percent	Undecided Percent	No Answer Percent
Independent	56.5	17.6	21.2	4.7
Catholic	23.4	60.9	14.8	.9
Methodist	37.2	43.5	18.2	1.1
Presbyterian	42.9	40.0	17.1	
Episcopalian	47.9	23.3	27.4	1.4
Congregational	44.7	30.8	24.5	
Lutheran	29.3	50.0	20.7	
Baptist	28.2	51.9	18.2	1.7
Mormon	14.9	78.5	6.2	.4
"Protestant"	46.5	32.6	2 9	
Total Non-Jewish	31.3	50.5	17.3	.9
Jewish	6.0	84.0	9.3	.7

7. Does the question of a future life worry you considerably?

	Yes Percent	No Percent	Undecided Percent	No Answer Percent
Independent	14.1	75.3	9.4	1.2
Catholic	26.6	62.7	9.9	.9
Methodist	16.4	74.0	9.7	
Presbyterian	8.6	85.7	2.9	2.9
Episcopalian	12.3	74.0	12.3	
Congregational	10.1	78.4	11.5	
Lutheran	20.7	63.8	15.5	
Baptist	29.3	59.7	10.5	.6
Mormon	13.5	80.7	5.5	.4
"Protestant"	18.6	69.8	11.6	
Total Non-Jewish	18.6	71.3	9.6	.5
Jewish	21.3	62.0	14.0	2.7

8. Would you prefer to know about the future life positively, or would you prefer to have it left a matter of faith or belief?

	Know Positively Percent	Faith or Belief Percent	No Answer Percent
Independent	51.8	43.5	4.7
Catholic	43.8	54.1	1.9
Methodist	32.7	65.8	1.5
Presbyterian	37.1	60.0	2.9
Episcopalian	23.3	76.7	
Congregational	31.7	67.3	1.0
Lutheran	34.5	65.5	
Baptist	31.5	66.9	1.7
Mormon	51.3	47.3	1.1
"Protestant"	27.9	65.1	7.0
Total Non-Jewish	39.6	58.5	1.7
Jewish	36.0	59.3	4.7

69

9. Do you feel that religious observances by the living can somehow benefit the state of those already dead?

	Yes Percent	No Percent	Undecided Percent	No Answer Percent
Independent	11.8	80.0	5.9	2.4
Catholic	65.7	18.2	15.0	.9
Methodist	11.9	71.0	16.7	. '
Presbyterian	8.6	74.3	17.1	
Episcopalian	13.7	65.8	20.5	
Congregational	7.2	78.8	13.5	.5
Lutheran	8.6	81.0	10.3	
Baptist	13.3	66.9	19.9	
Mormon	67.6	25.8	5.5	1.1
"Protestant"	18.6	69.8	11.6	
Total Non-Jewish	34.5	51.0	13.7	.7
Jewish	38.0	49.3	10.7	2.0

10. Is it your personal belief that there will be a future existence of some kind after death?

	Yes Percent	No Percent	Undecided Percent	No Answer Percent
Independent	25.9	54.1	18.8	1.2
Catholic	77.5	9.0	12.4	.9
Methodist	61.0	13.0	25.7	
Presbyterian	48.6	25.7	22.9	2.9
Episcopalian	52.1	20.5	27.4	
Congregational	49.5	19.7	29.8	.5
Lutheran	69.0	20.7	10.3	
Baptist	70.7	11.6	16.0	.6
Mormon	92.0	1.5	5.5	.4
"Protestant"	48.8	27.9	23.3	
Total Non-Jewish	65.7	15.0	18.0	.7
Jewish	65.3	16.7	15.3	2.0

11. Do you feel that capital punishment is warranted under any circumstances?

	Yes Percent	No Percent	Undecided Percent	No Answer Percent
Independent	35.3	48.2	12.9	3.5
Catholic	43.1	38.0	17.2	1.7
Methodist	29.7	53.2	14.9	1.1
Presbyterian	45.7	37.1	17.1	
Episcopalian	35.6	49.3	15.1	
Congregational	38.5	43.8	16.3	1.4
Lutheran	39.7	44.8	13.8	1.7
Baptist	32.0	40.3	26.5	1.1
Mormon	58.5	24.4	16.7	.4
"Protestant"	46.5	34.9	16.3	2.3
Total Non-Jewish	40.4	41.0	16.8	1.4
Jewish	42.0	34.7	19.3	3.3

12. Do you approve of mercy killing in cases of extreme suffering?

	No Percent	Yes Percent	In Some Cases Percent	If Self Administered Percent	No Answer Percent
Independent	15.3	31.8	27.1	18.8	7.6
Catholic	53.2	17.4	15.9	11.2	2.4
Methodist	32.7	13.4	22.7	26.8	4.1
Presbyterian	31.4	22.9	17.1	17.1	11.4
Episcopalian	23.3	23.2	34.2	16.4	2.7
Congregational	24.0	23.1	34.6	15.4	2.9
Lutheran	36.2	22.4	17.2	22.4	
Baptist	44.2	13.8	26.5	12.7	2.8
Mormon	56.4	10.2	19.3	9.8	4.0
"Protestant"	23.3	30.2	27.9	14.0	4.7
Total Non-Jewish	40.9	17.6	22.1	15.2	3.9
Jewish	47.3	12.0	22.0	16.0	2.7

71

13. Have your religious experiences in general served to increase or decrease fear toward your own death?

	Increase Percent	Decrease Percent	No Influence Percent	No Answer Percent
Independent	12.9	20.0	63.5	3.5
Catholic	23.4	57.1	18.2	1.3
Methodist	7.8	59.5	30.9	1.5
Presbyterian	5.7	60.0	34.3	
Episcopalian	5.5	58.9	34.2	
Congregational	5.3	51.9	40.4	2.4
Lutheran	17.2	63.8	19.0	
Baptist	13.3	56.9	29.3	.6
Mormon	4.4	85.8	9.5	.4
"Protestant"	9.3	55.8	32.6	2.3
Total Non-Jewish	12.1	59.0	27.4	1.3
Jewish	8.0	60.7	30.7	.7

14. Which of the following best described you?

	Death was never explained to me in childhood Percent	No memories of being exposed to death in childhood Percent	Questions were generally Answered in childhood Percent	No Answer Percent
Independent	24.7	16.5	47.1	10.6
Catholic	11.8	14.4	70.8	2.8
Methodist	13.8	19.7	62.5	3.3
Presbyterian	14.3	20.0	65.7	
Episcopalian	9.6	17.8	72.6	
Congregational	9.1	15.4	71.6	3.8
Lutheran	8.6	24.1	65.5	1.7
Baptist	12.2	13.8	71.3	2.8
Mormon	4.7	12.0	81.5	1.5
"Protestant"	14.0	18.6	60.5	7.0
Total Non-Jewish	11.3	15.1	69.9	3.1
Jewish	18.0	24.0	54.7	2.7

15. If you contracted a fatal illness, do you feel that you would want to be told you would most likely die?

	Yes Percent	No Percent	Undecided Percent	No Answer Percent
Independent	72.9	14.1	10.6	2.4
Catholic	79.4	12.2	7.3	.9
Methodist	70.3	16.7	10.4	2.2
Presbyterian	74.3	11.4	11.4	2.9
Episcopalian	79.5	9.6	11.0	
Congregational	68.8	13.5	16.3	1.4
Lutheran	72.4	22.4	5.2	
Baptist	58.6	24.9	15.5	1.1
Mormon	78.9	8.4	11.6	1.1
"Protestant"	60.5	27.9	11.6	
Total Non-Jewish	71.9	14.6	11.4	1.9
Jewish	55.3	24.0	19.3	1.3

16. Do you anticipate reunion with your loved ones in an afterlife?

	Yes Percent	No Percent	Undecided Percent	No Answer Percent
Independent	16.5	60.0	20.0	2.4
Catholic	52.8	18.7	27.9	.6
Methodist	40.9	25.3	32.0	1.5
Presbyterial	42.9	37.1	17.1	2.9
Episcopalian	28.8	27.4	42.5	1.4
Congregational	34.1	29.3	36.1	.5
Lutheran	51.7	24.1	22.4	
Baptist	52.5	17.7	29.8	
Mormon	90.2	4.0	5.5	.4
"Protestant"	34.9	39.5	23.3	2.3
Total Non-Jewish	49.5	23.6	25.8	.9
Jewish	34.7	24.0	39.3	2.0

17. Have you ever had a feeling that you were somehow in the presence of God?

	I'm sure I have Percent	I think I have Percent	No Percent	No Answer Percent
Independent	5.9	20.0	70.6	3.5
Catholic	40.8	39.7	17.4	1.9
Methodist	31.6	46.5	20.8	.7
Presbyterian	28.6	42.9	28.6	
Episcopalian	27.4	53.4	17.8	1.4
Congregational	27.4	44.2	26.9	1.4
Lutheran	41.4	39.7	19.0	
Baptist	37.6	45.9	15.5	1.1
Mormon	47.3	28.4	22.9	1.5
"Protestant"	41.9	23.3	32.6	2.3
Total Non-Jewish	35.2	39.6	23.2	1.8
Jewish	40.0	42.7	14.7	2.7

18. Have you ever had a feeling of being punished by God for something you have done?

	I'm Sure I have Percent	I think I have Percent	No Percent	No Answer Percent
Independent	7.1	16.5	72.9	3.5
Catholic	30.7	42.1	26.0	.9
Methodist	18.6	43.5	36.1	1.5
Presbyterian	22.9	40.0	37.1	
Episcopalian	11.0	42.5	45.2	1.4
Congregational	15.9	42.8	40.4	1.0
Lutheran	29.3	46.6	24.1	
Baptist	33.7	39.8	26.0	.6
Mormon	31.3	30.5	37.8	.4
"Protestant"	30.2	20.9	46.5	2.3
Total Non-Jewish	24.2	38.7	35.3	1.3
Jewish	38.7	41.3	17.3	2.0

19. What is your evaluation of the statement that the devil actually exists?

	Completely True Percent	Probably True Percent	Probably Not True Percent	Definitely Not True Percent	No Answer Percent
Independent	4.7	12.9	24.7	51.8	5.9
Catholic	37.1	35.0	17.2	6.4	3.9
Methodist	16.7	25.3	34.2	21.2	2.2
Presbyterian	11.4	28.6	25.7	31.4	2.9
Episcopalian	4.1	17.8	41.1	30.1	6.8
Congregational	3.8	15.4	41.3	35.6	3.8
Lutheran	27.6	36.2	17.2	17.2	1.7
Baptist	31.5	39.8	14.9	10.5	3.3
Mormon	84.4	9.8	3.6	1.8	.4
'Protestant"	27.9	7.0	41.9	18.6	4.7
Total Non-Jewish	32.5	23.0	22.2	18.6	3.4
Jewish	9.3	11.3	31.3	40.0	8.0

20. Which of the following best describes your general reaction when you think most seriously about God?

	Strong Fear Percent	Moderate Fear Percent	Slight Fear Percent	No Fear Percent	No Answer Percent
Independent	2.4	9.4	21.2	61.2	5.9
Catholic	11.8	25.5	22.7	38.2	1.7
Methodist	6.3	16.7	21.6	53.2	1.1
Presbyterian	8.6	11.4	17.1	62.9	
Episcopalian	2.7	12.3	26.0	57.5	1.4
Congregational	3.8	15.4	22.6	56.7	1.0
Lutheran	31.0	19.0	22.4	27.6	
Baptist	29.3	21.5	21.0	28.2	
Mormon	6.2	16.0	24.7	52.4	.7
"Protestant"	7.0	11.6	16.3	65.1	
Total Non-Jewish	10.5	18.8	22.0	47.1	1.3
Jewish	28.0	30.0	19.3	18.7	4.0

21. Which of the following statements comes closest to what you believe about God?

1. I know God really exists and I have no doubts about it.
2. While I have doubts, I feel that I do believe in God.
3. I find myself believing in God some of the time, but not at other times.
4. I don't believe in a personal God, but I do believe in a higher power of some kind.
5. I don't know whether there is a God and I don't believe there is any way to find out.
6. I don't believe in God.

	#1 Percent	#2 Percent	#3 Percent	#4 Percent	#5 Percent	#6 Percent	No Answer Percent
Independent	7.1	10.6	8.2	18.8	27.1	23.5	4.7
Catholic	53.2	30.7	5.4	5.6	3.6	.6	.6
Methodist	34.6	40.9	8.6	7.1	5.9	1.5	1.1
Presbyterian	28.6	40.0	2.9	11.4	14.3	2.9	
Episcopalian	26.0	42.5	15.1	6.8	6.8	0.0	2.7
Congregational	24.5	35.6	13.0	13.5	8.2	2.9	2.4
Lutheran	46.6	36.2	8.6	5.2	3.4	0.0	
Baptist	50.8	35.9	5.5	2.8	2.8	.6	1.7
Mormon	81.5	13.1	1.5	.7	2.5	.4	.4
"Protestant"	44.2	27.9	2.3	7.0	4.7	9.3	4.7
Total Non-Jewish	45.7	30.2	7.3	7.4	5.5	1.9	1.8
Jewish	57.3	24.0	6.7	5.3	2.7	0.0	4.0

22. Please indicate which of the following best expresses your concept
    of immortality?
    1. Biological (through one's children).
    2. Social (through work accomplishments that live on in the thoughts
       of the living).
    3. Transcendental (belief that life is but the pre-condition of the
       "true" life yet to come.
    4. Don't believe in immortality of any sort. Death is the end.
    5. Other. (Specify).

	#1 Percent	#2 Percent	#3 Percent	#4 Percent	#5 Percent	No Answer Percent
Independent	8.2	41.2	8.2	35.3	3.5	3.5
Catholic	5.8	13.7	61.2	8.2	7.1	4.1
Methodist	14.1	23.8	39.0	11.2	7.1	4.8
Presbyterian	11.4	37.1	34.3	14.3	2.9	
Episcopalian	15.1	31.5	27.4	12.3	9.6	4.1
Congregational	14.4	30.8	26.9	12.5	11.5	3.4
Lutheran	8.6	10.3	65.5	5.2	8.6	1.7
Baptist	10.5	19.3	53.0	10.5	3.3	3.3
Mormon	3.3	4.4	68.7	1.1	21.8	.7
"Protestant"	18.6	27.9	27.9	7.0	11.6	7.0
Total Non-Jewish	9.8	18.9	46.8	11.1	9.5	3.9
Jewish	20.7	16.7	35.3	10.7	12.0	4.0

23. How Would you describe your health history?

	Excellent Percent	Generally Good Percent	Average Percent	Poor Percent	No Answer Percent
Independent	34.1	45.9	11.8	4.7	3.5
Catholic	49.8	42.3	6.4	.6	.9
Methodist	48.0	39.0	11.5	1.5	
Presbyterian	60.0	37.1	2.9	0.0	
Episcopalian	69.9	27.4	2.7	0.0	
Congregational	51.9	39.9	7.2	.5	.5
Lutheran	48.3	43.1	8.6	0.0	
Baptist	36.5	52.5	8.8	2.2	
Mormon	69.1	27.6	2.2	.7	.4
"Protestant"	48.8	30.2	20.9	0.0	
Total Non-Jewish	51.8	39.2	6.6	1.1	.9
Jewish	46.7	46.7	4.7	2.0	

CHAPTER 9

DEATH CONTROL

Glenn M. Vernon

ABSTRACT--What appears to be an emerging public acceptance
of death control has followed a meaning-of-death developmental
sequence from (1) supernatural control to (2) biological control
to (3) social-symbolic control. The "social death" concept is
beginning to take its place beside the "biological death" concept.
Belief that biological factors should control death, which incorporates belief in instinctive self-preservation and instinctive
fear of death, is being replaced by interpretations summarized
in the statement that the behavior of an individual as he confronts
death and dying is in response to symbols (meaning) and is relative to the audience and the situation. People are increasingly
questioning the beliefs that (1) biological preservation is inherently of greater worth than preservation of the social-symbolic
image of the dying, which includes self-definitions productive
of dignity, and (2) whether bureaucratic hospital dying is always
preferable to dying at home.

Sociological and common sense interpretations of human behavior have
followed a broad historical pattern. Early interpretations were heavily theological in nature, explaining human behavior largely on the basis of some supernatural
variables. Man was seen as being largely controlled by God or other supernatural
forces. Theological interpretations were gradually replaced by biological interpretations in which man's behavior was viewed as being controlled by biological
factors such as instincts, drives, mind, and conscience. Since these "things"
were believed to be located inside the individual, the resulting interpretation of
human behavior turned out to be individualistic in nature. The individual was
seen as the behaving entity, with his behavior being caused by factors inside him.
In essence, explanations taking into account outer space were replaced with explanations taking into account inner space. Both, however, involved metaphysical
constructs that greatly reduced the utility thereof for scientific research. It is
as difficult to study God scientifically in outer space as it is to study the mind or
instincts in inner space. An increase in the use of the scientific method has
served to reduce the use of such metaphysical concepts and consequently has
encouraged a search for a more adequate model of behavior.

Whereas supernatural determinism deifies God and His power, biological determinism, in essence, deifies biology. When supernatural and biological factors were integrated into some configuration of meaning, God was usually interpreted as being on the side of biology. This is, of course, not surprising, since man's biology was viewed as being the creation of God.

The third broad orientation to be developed has emphasized the social-symbolic nature of behavior which can be summarized in the statement that the behavior of the individual (I) is in response to symbols (S) and is relative to the audience (A) and relative to the situation (S), represented by ISAS. (For further discussion of the ISAS paradigm see Vernon, 1972.) The concern here is primarily with the behavior of interacting individuals, not the behavior of some internal sub-individual biological entity. The orientation emphasizes the importance of distinguishing between (1) any biological factor or condition per se, and (2) what one does about that biological condition. A biological condition is obviously biological and is influenced by, while it has influence on, other related biological factors. What one does about it, however, stems from the meaning attributed to it, and this is socially constructed.

The three stages can be outlined as follows:

Supernatural Determinism	Biological Determinism	Social-symbolic Orientation
Supernatural predestination	Biological predestination	Socially constructed moral-value decisions
outer space orientation	inner space orientation	"social-symbolic space" orientation

In all of these stages efforts have been made to determine the responsibility for human acts. Responsibility was typically located with the factors that were interpreted as controlling behavior. A theological interpretation puts the responsibility primarily upon God. Biological determinism places the responsibility in man's biological makeup. In both cases, the theological doctrine of predestination is applicable, suggesting that nonhuman factors predetermine, preprogram, or force man to behave in particular ways. They control man. The social-symbolic interpretation places part of the responsibility for acts upon the interacting individuals who construct their behavior. Part of the responsibility is located in the society in which the behavior occurs. Part of it is related to the ancestors who created the symbol system or culture inherited by the living. Another part of the responsibility is placed on other situational factors involved. From the social-symbolic perspective there is a scapegoat element in both of the other perspectives. If God or biology is responsible for behavior, man himself, individually or collectively cannot be held responsible.

79

Human behavior is an especially complex phenomenon. Clearly, there are nonhuman factors involved, which may be interpreted as being supernatural, such as God the Father, or nonhuman natural forces, such as "Mother Nature." Equally clearly, biological factors are involved, as are social-symbolic factors. Students of human behavior are still trying to determine the relative influences of each of these major variables. Today many of our interpretations of human behavior contain a heavy proportion of biological deterministic concepts. Traces of biological deterministic thinking, for instance, are incorporated in the language that most of us use in statements such as: (1) "He has a good heart;" (2) "I have a feeling that such-and-such is going to happen;" and (3) "It was a gut reaction." Likewise, the following widely used concepts all incorporate biological deterministic dimensions: instincts, drives, mind, attitude (defined as an internal predisposition to act), habits, memory, and conscience.

Using this perspective of changing interpretations of human behavior (theological→biological→social-symbolic) this article presents an analysis of what seems to be appropriately labeled death control. What appears to be an emerging acceptance of death control has followed the developmental sequences of the acceptance of birth control and appears to incorporate many of the same dimensions. A supernatural deterministic interpretation of death places God in control of the basic process. A person's death is controlled by supernatural factors. A person dies at the convenience of God, or when God calls him home, or decides that his time for death has arrived. From a biological deterministic orientation, death has been perceived as being biological in nature. Biology is in control. The biological causes of death have been given primary emphasis and frequently have been interpreted as the only (or at least the major) causes of death. The fact that, biologically, death is inevitable has been incorporated in many interpretations of life, in some of which it has been identified as the major factor involved in the meaning of life.

As interpretations of behavior have moved from emphasis upon biological factors to emphasis upon social-symbolic factors, we are beginning to accept and utilize the concept of social death. Social death contrasts with biological death. Biological death involves the termination of biological functioning, namely of the heart or the brain. The body ceases to function. Social death, by way of contrast, is a condition in which the individual, although biologically alive, is unable to function in any meaningful social manner. The individual is incapable of symbolic interaction. With the gradual increased awareness of the importance of social death, efforts are being made to evaluate the relative importance and consequences of these two types of death.

80

The developing awareness of social death has been related to increased awareness of social factors involved in one way or another in biological death. These involve the development and use of heart transplants and kidney machines. Other social factors influencing death are war, pollution, type of occupation, type of diet, and primary or love relationships. There are many social factors involved in any biological death.

Biological deterministic interpretations of behavior have incorporated the premise that human individuals instinctively (biologically) strive to preserve biological life. Although there is no supporting scientific proof, widespread acceptance has been given to the belief that there is an instinct for self-preservation. The following sequence of events may have been involved in the development of this concept. Biologists and physicians have been aware that at the sub-individual level (at the organ level, the cell level, or the biological system level) unlearned or instinctive (biologically given) factors do function to maintain life. For instance, the normal human body does not have to be taught to increase the flow of adrenalin under certain conditions. If awareness of such sub-individual behavior is generalized to the individual level, one can logically conclude that the individual behaves in the manner of these sub-individual elements and instinctively (in an unlearned manner) strives to preserve life. What is logical, however, is not always true.

This myth of instinctive individual self-preservation has been widely accepted. It has been accepted, however, in the face of considerable contradictory evidence. In the first place, no one has ever found such a biological phenomenon anywhere inside an individual or anywhere in his biology. What appears to have happened is that the belief that such a biological instinct does exist has led to the symbolic construction of a metaphysical construct, namely self-preservation instinct, to which behavior can be attributed even if it cannot be empirically demonstrated. Actually, if there were an instinct for self-preservation or if human individuals instinctively did those things necessary to preserve life, there would be no need for medical and allied professions. As has been suggested, at the individual level behavior is in response to symbols, meaning or knowledge. Thus, when the human being decides that there is something biologically wrong, he typically consults the expert who informs him of the meaning of his condition and further tells him what to do about that condition. What he does is in response to these symbols. Human beings do not automatically know what is wrong with them. They typically consult experts to find out.

If the belief that humans instinctively strive to preserve themselves is accepted, there is little likelihood of being concerned with any aspects of death control. It also appears that the belief in instinctive self-preservation has contributed to the belief that keeping an individual biologically alive is of greater importance or takes precedence over keeping the individual socially alive. To state the same point in reverse, biological death is evaluated as being more serious than social death. It has also led to the conclusion that maintaining an individual biologically is more important than maintaining a symbolic self definition. If it is believed that this instinct for self-preservation is somehow God-given or that it is supernatural in origin, this belief could be used to support the high evaluation of biological preservation. God intended that man would so behave.

However, a social-symbolic interpretation of behavior rejects the myth of instinctive self-preservation, indicating that symbolic definitions or know-ledge intervene between biological factors and individual behavior. Behavior of an individual is in response to symbols (meaning) rather than directly caused by biological factors. From this perspective an individual may want to preserve his life: on the other hand, he may want to take his life. The occurrence of suicide indicates the success with which such a desire can be accomplished.

If individuals instinctively strive to preserve their life, it would be hard, in fact, to explain the behavior of the GI in Viet Nam or the behavior of the reli-gious martyr. Actually, the empirical evidence suggests that for practically everybody there is some cause for which they would give their life. Dorothy Lee (1959), an anthropologist, has suggested that she can find a record of no society in which self-preservation is the thing most highly valued. It is true that the majority of individuals do strive to preserve their lives under most conditions. Behavior however is always relative to the situation, and if under some condi-tions they are willing to give their lives and do, in fact, give their lives, it appears that a biological deterministic explanation (namely instinctive self-preservation) is inadequate to explain this variation. An interpretation which emphasizes the social-symbolic nature of such behavior is more adequate. The behavior of the individual is in response to symbols and is relative to the audience and the situation (ISAS). Given the right set of meaning, validated by appropriate audiences, in the appropriate situations, most individuals will behave in ways contrary to self-preservation. The fact that the majority of individuals do, under most conditions, actively strive to preserve life does not require a biological deterministic interpretation.

A biological deterministic interpretation of behavior also seems to have contributed to the widespread myth that human beings instinctively fear death. This, of course, is related to the item we have just discussed about the myth of instinctive self-preservation. Interpretations of human behavior provided by many religionists, as well as some social scientists, support the belief in the existence of an instinctive fear of death. With reference to fears of death, it is

important to distinguish between fear of death in general as an abstract phenomenon and fear of one's own death. Research evidence supports the premise that
each is a distinctive type of fear. There is, most likely, no necessary relationship between them. Research evidence does support the conclusion that there is,
in fact, a widespread fear of death. The existence of such a phenomenon, however, does not require a biological deterministic explanation.

Social-symbolic interpretation suggests that death can be feared or accepted. As with all phenomena, death can be evaluated in any number of different ways. For most people the fear of living under certain conditions is stronger
than the fear of death. Generally older individuals are more fearful of living in
an incapacitated dependent condition than they are fearful of dying. Fear of death
has been found to be related to many types of social variables. Members of different church groups evidence different fears of death. Research evidence also
suggests that physicians have stronger fears of death than do non-physicians.
Fear of death is a social-symbolic, rather than a biologically given, phenomenon.

As has been suggested, the preservation of the biological being has usually
been evaluated as being of greater worth than the preservation of the social being.
Be-ing biologically is more important than be-ing socially and symbolically.
Most people appear to accept this conclusion without any question and without
any difficulty. However, as awareness is increased of the distinction between
biological death and social-symbolic death, these unquestioned assumptions are
being subjected to more critical evaluation. The fact that older people are more
fearful of living in an incapacitated dependent state than they are of dying suggests
that to these people in their condition the social-symbolic life is more important
than biological life. The fact that suicide does occur likewise underscores the
point that for certain individuals living under certain conditions is of less value
than taking their lives. The whole phenomenon of face-saving suggests that preserving one's self-definitions or one's self-image is very important to most
people. Thus, many conclude that "if I can't respect myself and live, I would
rather respect myself and die."

The interaction paradigm (ISAS) emphasizes the relativity of actual decisions and behavior. When value decisions are considered alone without relating
them to actual behavior, it is easy to treat them as though they were in fact absolute or unchanging. There are no other factors involved that are likely to
change them or to have a modifying influence upon them. To consider value decisions alone emphasizes the "Symbol" dimensions of the paradigm, and ignores
the other three major variables.

However, when the other variables are taken into account, as they are in all actual behavior, the evaluation of life or death (or any other phenomenon) by one individual is relative to the audience toward which his behavior is directed and is relative to the situation. Abstract symbolic concepts (ideals) always lose something when they are applied in actual behavior. Abstract death is quite different from an actual death. The point being made here is that in the current situation, evaluations of death are changing. The possibility of greater death control is being given consideration.

For instance, questions are starting to be raised about the current patterns of dying in the bureaucratic hospital. Does such dying permit the individual to die with the same degree of dignity that could be accorded him if his last time was spent with those near and dear to him in a more intimate personal relationship? The value question involved is whether a shorter time for living with one's family is of greater worth than a longer life in a hospital. Such questions emphasize the importance of social death.

It is somewhat paradoxical that Christians frequently condemn "death control" by invoking religious interpretations, while at the same time they accept the basic premise of their religion that Christ voluntarily and freely gave His life (controlled His own death). One of the major Christian rituals celebrates this voluntary death, and an oft-quoted Christian statement is "greater love hath no man than He lay down His life for others."

With reference to death control, those who voluntarily and rationally decide to do or not to do something that hastens death are frequently accused of "playing God." If one means by the phrase "playing God" that something is done which influences the subsequent death, then those who decide to prolong life by taking or giving drugs, securing an operation, by "heroic efforts" are likewise "playing God." Actually, in terms of the biological death of most individuals it is safe to say that society does "play God" since many social factors influence the death of most people. This point is raised in the following quotation:

In the Hippocratic Oath doctors are admonished to preserve life until the end. Yet physicians are committed toward the alleviation of suffering. Some doctors point out that it is useless to try to preserve life knowing that the extension of life will bring to the patient strange and new illnesses, and possibly even greater suffering. Shouldn't a person be allowed to die when they are ready to die? Old age breeds illnesses peculiar to the aging, such as arteriosclerosis and senile psychosis. Should doctors prolong the life of a patient knowing that the second condition may even be worse than the first? (Academy Reporter, 1968)

84

Physicians and others at times justify prolonging biological life as long as possible by referring to cases where remarkable recoveries have been made. A question frequently ignored in such justifications, however, is how many cases of biologically-alive-but-socially-dead people does one such remarkable recovery cost? In such cases the human cost of family anguish, financial and other social problems frequently is very high.

If one starts out with a biological deterministic orientation, decisions about death are typically made by experts in the area of biology. In many respects the individual dies at the convenience of the doctor and the hospital. Decisions as to what will be communicated to the dying individual about his impending death are likewise primarily made by the experts in the realm of biology. To distinguish biological death from social death and to emphasize, or at least recognize, the social-symbolic dimensions of dying leads, in certain respects at least, to a greater willingness to let the individual control his own death. In such cases the individual dies at his convenience or possibly at the convenience of those who are significant to him in a primary love relationship. Greater likelihood of dying with dignity is involved. Such dignity, of course, is defined by the individual involved. Under certain conditions, dying in a hospital may provide the maximum of dignity and positive self-definition. If one is to die defining himself as being a worthy, dignified individual, it is important that his significant others validate this definition by treating him in the appropriate manner. If this cannot be accomplished by dying at home, then other arrangements would seem to be preferable. Every society evaluates different types of death and dying differently. Some type of individual death control permits the individual to invoke his own evaluative system.

Dying with dignity may also involve a period of reminiscing, in which time is spent re-interpreting, re-integrating, re-analyzing and re-editing (symbolically reconstructing) one's life so that it can be seen as an entity and evaluated accordingly. Use of a social-symbolic interpretation is more likely than use of a biological interpretation to lead to therapy and counseling of the dying individual. When factors such as these which are associated with social death are emphasized, individuals are more likely to be granted the opportunity to engage in what they consider to be appropriate "goodbyes."

Kalish (1965) suggests that the following four guidelines should be taken into account in value decisions about the control of death. His guidelines reflect value definitions, which he accepts and which he would like to have adopted by society at large.

1. A man's life belongs to him, not to the state, the church, or the family; not to the medical profession, the mental health movement, the educational system, or the economic system. A man's death then also belongs to him and not to other agencies, institutions, or individuals. While such a statement overlooks the social nature of man, it indicates that decisions about the life and death of an individual should not be made without involving the one affected in the decision-making process.

2. The maximum preservation of biological life need not be an overriding value. This is recognized implicitly in laws regarding capital punishment, compulsory draft for active participation in military battles, etc. We often seem more reluctant to recognize it in the final weeks of a terminally ill patient. A corollary is that neither should physical pain, fear and anxiety, or emotional distress be overriding.

3. Dignity, physical discomfort, and human relationships are just as important for the person with a few hours left to live as for an individual with a life expectancy of 50 years. Dignity is not synonymous with stoicism or quiet resignation; physical comfort is not synonymous with heavy sedation; human relationships do not consist of perfunctory visits from the family and cheerful falsehoods received from the hospital staff.

4. Since individual differences occur throughout the life-span, they obviously extend throughout the dying process and after.

Douglas (1967) in his discussion of suicide, also indicates that longevity need not be the overriding value definition involved in death behavior. He points out that, at the time when free will and individualistic interpretations of behavior were strongly endorsed, suicide was usually evaluated in highly moralistic terms. The one committing suicide was immoral and was so treated by society. However, as an interpretation emphasizing the social nature of behavior has been accepted the individual is seen as but one element in a larger configuration of interacting elements. Interpretations of suicide have consequently changed. The individual who commits suicide has been defined increasingly as a victim rather than a perpetrator of a crime or sin. Definitions of suicide, including the moralistic interpretations related to or involved in it, have taken a broader perspective; and, while the individual has not been completely absolved of blame or causal connection, he has been viewed as not solely responsible for his own death.

The same point can be made about death in general. The realization that there are many social factors involved in any death and that any of the factors or some configuration of them can be evaluated separately from the death element per se has no doubt influenced society to modify the widely held value definition that life should be preserved at all costs and under all circumstances.

Suicide in the abstract is still widely condemned, but a particular suicide is usually interpreted in terms of the situational factors involved. Most particular suicides today, when evaluated as social acts, are not morally condemned. The same interpretation may be true of death in general. The preservation of life in the abstract is no doubt still highly valued. The maximum preservation of a particular life in a particular situation seems to be increasingly subject to elements of doubt.

The American society appears to be changing in the direction of greater approval of death control. When college-age respondents were asked (Vernon, 1970) "Do you approve of mercy killings in cases of extreme suffering?" they answered as follows:

	Number	Percent
No	614	40.9
Yes	365	17.6
Yes, in some cases	332	22.1
Yes, but only if the lethal agent is self-administered or requested by the patient	229	15.2

The majority approved under certain conditions.

Many social factors combine to facilitate any change. Awareness that, within limits, death can be controlled has been established. A willingness to accept responsibility for a particular death is not extensive. A willingness to extend the responsibility in part to the individual most directly involved in the very personal act of dying is even less extensive. The American society does seem to be moving in that direction. Pandey (1971) indicates for instance that "Our understanding of death and control over it have suddenly expanded to such a point that the religious and philosophical buttresses of our classical systems of human values as well as many time-honored scientific concepts have become antiquated."

Changes in definitions about life and death are difficult to achieve, since they involve many of the basic value definitions of a society that are usually taken for granted. Opposition to such change, then, will be in evidence for many years. The direction of change seems to be established and will most likely continue.

We have identified three major types of interpretations of human death control: supernatural control (determinism), biological control (determinism), and social-symbolic control. As far as actual physical death is concerned, it appears that the immediate causes are largely outside the individual and are social and symbolic in nature. What then has happened to the factors included

87

in earlier interpretations? It appears that the variables are still being taken into account, but that the way in which they are seen as being involved in death is changing.

The supernatural factor is increasingly seen as being involved in the answers to questions about the origin of death, the necessity for death among humans, and the justification for the existence of death in general.

Biological factors are seen as being involved in the actual process or in the mechanics of death. Such factors are necessary but not sufficient to explain the actual death.

Social-symbolic factors then are seen as the immediate causes of the actual biological death.

All three factors can be incorporated into interpretations of death. Each, however, is involved at a different level. Control of actual-death factors, then, is largely a social-symbolic phenomenon. Increased future acceptance of death control appears likely.

REFERENCES

Academy Reporter
    1968   Vol. 13, No. 4, April. Academy of Religion and Mental Health, New York, N.Y.

Douglas, Jack D.
    1967   Social Meaning of Suicide. Princeton, N.J.: Princeton University Press.

Kalish, Richard A.
    1965   "The Aged and the Dying Process: The Inevitable Decision." Journal of Social Issues, 21: 87-96.

Lee, Dorothy
    1959   Freedom and Culture. New York: Prentice-Hall.

Pandey, Carol
    1971   "The Need for the Psychological Study of Clinical Death." Omega, 2: 1-9.

Vernon, Glenn M.
    1972   Human Interaction, 2nd ed. New York: The Ronald Press Co.

    1970   The Sociology of Death. New York: The Ronald Press Co.

CHAPTER 10

PERCEIVED MORALITY OF EUTHANASIA*

Glenn M. Vernon
University of Utah

The analysis of euthanasia provided herewith utilizes the Symbolic Interactionist (SI) Theory of human behavior. The nucleus of this approach is contained in the paradigm statement that the behavior of the Individual is in response to Symbols, is relative to the Audience and relative to the Situation. ISAS is a shorthand paradigm form.[1]

Death-related behavior including euthanasia is interpreted as being in response to symbols (meaning), relative to the audience and the situation. In basic symbolic and interaction components death-related behavior is no different from any other phenomenon. Humans create definitions thereof and socially construct (1) plans of action (script, blueprint, recipe, models) and (2) evaluations (validation, legitimation, motivation) justifying the script and the script-related behavior. Our primary concern here is with the validation of both the anti and the pro euthanasia positions.

The basic premises of Symbolic Interactionism which are germane to our analysis are capsulized as follows, being presented here in terms of death-related behavior.

1. The behavior of concern is interaction (social or group behavior) not internal biological or sub-individual behavior. Euthanasia is a social act involving interacting individuals.

2. The behavior of interacting individuals is in response to symbols (meaning or cognition) and is not determined biologically. The biological processes of dying or living do not determine what individuals do to cause death or what they do about death. Individuals respond to the labels they place upon death-related behavior and any other phenomenon involved. Efforts to achieve meaning consensus are constantly underway and most likely never completely successful.

3. Humans take into account two types of symbols: (1) symbols which have an empirical referent and which are used to identify selected aspects of the empirical world such as the biological parts of the human body and the body as a biological entity, and (2) non-referented symbols which have no referent or which do not re-present anything else. They present themselves. In the absence of biologically provided motivators or drives, non-referented symbols have as one major function the justification (motivation, legitimation) of behavior. Death-related behavior is in response to and influenced by both types.

4. Humans can see and experience what a label calls for even though the referent may not be empirically present. People can symbolically

_____

* Enlarged version of article in Journal of Contemporary Law. Vol. no. 2, Univ. of Utah, 1975.

provide elements missing in some configuration or system and take into account the whole configuration. One can respond to what he believes or real-izes is there rather than just what is there.

5. There is no inherent relationship between symbol and referent (that to which a symbol refers) except the human one. Humans decide which symbol will identify a particular referent. Such relationships are subject to change. The same symbols may be used to identify two or more different phenomena and the same phenomenon can be labeled with two or more different symbols. Various aspects of euthanasia are defined differently by different people.

6. Ignorance of certain aspects may be functional in the accomplishment of certain goals. Keeping society unaware of the extent to which euthanasia is practiced may help achieve certain goals.

7. Perception is always selective. The symbols used identify the aspect of death-related behavior to which attention is being given. Selectively paying attention to one configuration, involves selectively ignoring or "backgrounding" other phenomena.

8. The behaivor of the individual in response to any internal biological factor or the body as an entity, is in response to the labels used to identify it, rather than in direct response to the biological factor per se. Death-related behavior of individuals then is in response to (among other things) labels used to provide meaning and socially provided motive definitions (not biologically provided "motives") which utilize non-referented symbols to legitimate the behavior.

9. Decisions about death-related behavior are emergent. They have no prior existence "out there" or "in there." They can, however, achieve an existence independent of the individuals who make or create the decisions, in the form of laws, mores, and folkways which are part of the culture of the group. Such symbolic preservation is, in fact, necessary if human societies are to function and persist.

10. Humans can symbolically re-create or re-member the past and pre-create or pre-member the future and take these symbolic phenomena into account in the present. Doing so is necessary if society is to function and persist.

11. There is a meaningful distinction between (a) the decision (b) the decided about and (c) the deciders. With reference to values this is the distinction between (a) evaluations (b) evaluated and (c) evaluator.

Laws

Human behavior is in response to symbols. This permits us to symbolically introduce into on-going "now" behavior a re-membered or reconstituted past and a pre-membered or pre-created future. One of the technics which humans have developed to take their anticipated future into account in the present and to influence that future is to create symbolically what are variously called blurprints, recipies, scripts, maps, models or expectations. "Norm Definitions" is the sociological concept which includes these. Major types are the formal laws and informal folkways and mores. These specify how the as yet uncreated behavior of the future is expected to be performed. In essence, we pre-form behavior and then perform it. The analysis here focuses upon the norm definitions concerning euthanasia.

In making decisions, we typically make extensive use of the prescriptions which our ancestors pre-created, upon the assumption that they know what would be good for us today, even though the laws and related moral standards were created "back then." Today with reference to euthanasia, we are experiencing two basic problems. First, we are deciding whether we are willing to perform our death-related behavior in the manner that our ancestors per-formed it in the laws they created. Secondly, since we are also involved in per-forming behavior which will influence our own behavior tomorrow and the behavior of those growing up in our society, we are or should be concerned with matching our blueprints to the conditions of tomorrow, realizing that we can't be at all sure what that tomorrow will actually be.

Validation

Humans engage in behavior in response to the meaning which they create for whatever behavioral episode is underway. An important component of this meaning is the reasons provided for doing whatever is being done. These "reasons for doing" have been called legitimation, validation, evaluation or motivation. Humans are concerned not only with doing the "right thing" but with doing it for the right reasons. Euthanasia behavior then is related to euthanasia validation or legitimation. This is true of both accepting and rejecting behavior.

There are no inherent limitations as to how doing a given act (or not doing a given act) can be symbolically legitimated. Legitimation concepts and procedures are socially constructed. Euthanasia can be done or not done for many different reasons, or justified by many different justifications. Two broad questions of validation are whether it is moral and whether it is legal. Legality stems from desisions made according to some approved legal procedure and thus incorporated within the legal structure. Morality is not formally or legally created, but stems more from informal consensus. However, when compared with laws, the manner of creation in no way reduces the strength or importance thereof. Indeed, when laws are defined as immoral they are difficult to enforce.

Morality definitions are frequently reinforced by religious definitions. An act is both good and of God. High Intensity moral definitions can, in fact, be interpreted as being the major ingredient of religion, with the second typically being definitions of the supernatural.

There is no objective, empirical or scientific method by which the morality of euthanasia can be determined. Morality is socially constructed and hence always subject to change if those involved decide that change is appropriate and if the situation is appropriate.

The configuration of moral definitions applied to euthanasia is diverse. Those who approve provide what to them is ample moral justification for the practice. Those who disapprove do likewise. Review of the euthanasia literature permits us to identify the broad patterns of approval and disapproval which have been at various times created and accepted by various individuals and groups. The presentation made here is not an effort to endorse one and reject the other. We are concerned with identification of the validaiton definitions of both sides. The literature frequently includes case histories which are provided to support a particular position. Such cases are not considered here. Since we are concerned with matters of life and death, it is not surprising that the responses are frequently of an emotional nature.

Like everything else dying is a complex phenomenon with many interrelated dimensions. It is literally impossible for any given decision to take into account all dimensions thereof. Specific decisions selectively take into account aspects of the larger area of death which are then selectively responded to and selectively evaluated.

Decisions about euthanasia per se can be reached from selectively focusing upon any of a number of specific components. The components to which attention is acutally given may shift over time and even from case to case. General societal concern with specific components shifts over time.

Euthanasia may in fact be accepted or rejected not primarily because of any characteristic of euthanasia per se, but rather because some aspect of euthanasia is interpreted as being one case or illustration of some broader phenomenon. Thus euthanasia may be rejected because to do so is seen as defending an established religion or possibly defending ones's God. The concern may not be so much with the euthanasia per se as with the "religious package" one endorses.

Attention is now given to the major types of validation used by those who accept euthanasia. These are subdivided or categorized according to the component of the broader configuration taken into account. Sources which have developed these validations in greater detail are identified.

Pro Euthanasia Legitimation

Dignity of Individual -- Quality of Life

The quality of life is as important, if not more important, than mere quantity of life. Whether an individual is happy or miserable is an important consideration.

Dignity is an important component of both living and dying. Living without dignity, or being forced into an undignified death is of doubtful value. Maintaining self respect or a positive self image is a part of dignified living.

"Life not worth living" is a meaningful concept. There is such a thing. The worth of life or living is influenced by distress, illness, physical or mental handicaps or dispair. It is doubtful that certain procedures are prolonging life as much as delaying death. Is a person really "alive" if he can engage in no interaction with others? Is "living" as a vegetable really the type of living we want to preserve? (Bard and Fletcher 1968, Douglas 1967, Fletcher 1960, Freeman 1972, Callahue 1963, Kalish 1965, Paulson 1973, Vernon 1974, Wilkes 1972).

Shneidman (1974: 29) suggests that an "appropriate death" is appropriate to the individual's time of life, to his style of life, to his situation in life, to his mission (aspriation, goals, wishes) in life. It is appropriate to the significant others in his life. Weber (1973) concludes that respect for the dying person may demand that we stop the art of healing so that we can help the patient practice what medieval man called ars moriendi, the art of dying.

Importance of Individual Choice

The human ability to make intelligent choices is the most distinguishing human characteristic. This freedom of choice should be honored with reference to death. Not to grant to the individual the right of choice means that he is at the mercy of his biological functioning. God can be seen as working or "speaking" through intelligent human choices rather than only through biology, such as the failure of sick or wounded organs to function. Human dignity involves making personal choices. Making intelligent choices is a "spiritual" activity. Greater love hath no man than he by choice lay down his life for something considered to be of greater worth.

The behavior of the Stoics incorporated this orientation. When death seemed inevitable they chose it before someone else could inflict it upon them. (Dyck 1973, Maguire 1974, Tillich 1952.)

Body "ownership." The individual owns his own body and he therefore should make the major choices regarding that body. (Kalish 1965.)

Religious Components

Religious interpretations such as the following support euthanasia:
a. Preserving biological life at all costs may mean that we are in fact deifying biology or biological life rather than worshipping God. (Maguire 1974a, Sholin 1968.)

b. Euthanasia in certain situations can be interpreted as a manifestation of God's love and compassion. Not to relieve suffering

93

can be seen as sinful. (Fletcher 1973, Sholin 1969)

    c. Our moral fiber must be weak to permit certain instances of prolonging suffering without instituting euthanasia. Does it require more moral courage to prolong biological life under "undesirable" conditions or to permit death under certain conditions? (Fletcher 1973)

    d. Biblical supports include the following:

    Leviticus 24:17. He who kills a man should be put to death. This statement rejects one type of killing while endorsing another.

    Eccl. 3:2-3. There is "a time to be born and a time to die-- a time to kill and a time to heal."

    Genesis 1: 28. God gave man dominion "over every living thing that moveth upon the earth."

    e. The Catholic Encyclopedia and Pope Pius XII in 1957 indicate that there are cases in which heroic efforts to preserve life are not warranted. (Downing 1969, Miller 1960)

    f. The Book of Common Prayer translates "thou shalt not kill" as "thou shalt do no murder," and Prof. Joseph Fletcher of the Episcopal Theological School points out that in the original Hebrew, the commandment both in exodus and in Deuteronomy employs the verb "ratsach" which means "treacherous unlawful killing" and the New Testament references (Matthew, Luke and Romans)use the verb "pheneuo" also involving unlawfulness. (Moor 1966)

    G. If the Lord does not intend for humans to interfer in biological processes how can we justify interfering with the progress of diseases that may lead to death, or using anesethesia for operations, or even performing operations in the first place? (Williams 1973)

    H. Meserve (1975:5) writing from a religious perspective suggests that an euthanasia choice, like marriage, should not be made "unadvisedly or lightly." It should, like marriage, be made "reverently, discreetly, soberly and in the fear of God." Decisions in favor of euthanasia can be made "religiously."

Type of Ethics -- Absolute or Relative

    While humans can create, in the abstract, value definitions or ethics considered to be eternal and absolute, when value definitions are applied to specific individuals in interaction, with specific others (audiences) in specific situations (ISAS) absolute values always become relative. Decisions about euthanasia in specific cases (as contrasted with abstract) are always relative. There is no one factor which will in all situations override all others. (Fletcher 1973, Maguire 1974, Vernon 1974.)

    Wedge Fear. The so-called "wedge fear" is unwarranted. Accepting certain euthanasia practices does not necessarily lead to accepting a flood of other types of killing once the wedge has been established. Hitler did not engage in "mercy killing." He practiced merciless killing (Fletcher 1973)

    An absolute ethics perspective locates the origin of the ethic outside of man, in the supernatural or some other "inherent," non-human aspect. The "relativists" locate the origin in humans collectively. Neither sees humans as potentially able to function without value definitions. The difference is in the perspective with

94

reference to origin. This is an important difference, however.

The non-human world exists but the morality of any aspect thereof or of any act of man toward that world, does not exist in the empirical world. It exists in man's symbolic or "spiritual" world. The world per se and the in-world empirical objects react to each other. Humans act in response to the symbols or meaning used to re-present that world and to the symbols incorporated in symbolically pre-created futures.

Societal Concerns

Humans should be concerned with societal problems such as over population. Concern should be given to the economic and personal "costs" of prolonging, possibly in an expensive hospital setting, of "life" which has no chance of being anything but a "vegetable condition."

Medical Ethics

Established medical ethics do not necessarily reject euthanasia. The Hippocratic oath stresses the importance of relieving suffering as well as prolonging and protecting life. (Academy Reporter 1968, Williams 1973)

Pain

Painful dying should be avoided if possible. We should have concern and compassion for those who are painfully and terminally ill. Not to relieve painful suffering is sinful. (Dyck 1973)

Potential Recovery

Yes, theoretically there is a remote chance of recovery, but in many cases of recovery there is a high probability that other troubles will result, possibly prolonging living as a vegetable and prolonging agony if consciousness is regained. How many cases of prolonged suffering-agony does each case of "remarkable recovery" cost? Is the "trade-off" worth it? (Academy Reporter 1968)

Anti Euthanasia Legitimation

Diginity

While it is important for the dignity of humans that individuals be permitted to make moral choices, such choices are limited to refusing life-prolonging treatment, but not to initiating life-taking acts.

95

Religious Components

These validations may involve the defense of a religious component of a larger religious configuration, in addition to (or even to the exclusion of) euthanasia per se. People rejecting euthanasia may be defending rightiousness or "God's word" and may be "out to get" the enemies of religion.

"Playing God." For humans to engage in euthanasia is "playing God." God, not humans should control death. Humans should not attempt to usurp what is rightly God's. In the background may be the related belief that individuals and maybe society will be punished for not "staying in their place." (Dyck 1973, Williams, 1973)

Euthanasia is religiously and morally wrong. Exodus 20: 13 specifies "Thou shalt not kill." The most important value involved is goodness itself or God. Humans are not perfect, they, therefore, need restraints upon any human decisions as to who deserves to live or deserves to die. Society must protect those who cannot protect themselves.

In Judaism there is no history of infanticide. The Jews reared the blind and the crippled. Jewish parents had no power of life or death. Rabbi William F. Rosenblum of the Central Conference of American Rabbis representing Reformed Judiasm has proclained "It is a maxim of Judaism that one must do everything humally possible to prolong a life."

The Judaic-Christian heritage is reflected in the medical ethic which requires preserving life at all costs. (Dyck 1973, Encyclopedia Americana 1968, Freeman 1972, Miller 1960, Time March 13, 1972)

Type of Ethics -- Absolute or Relative

An euthanasia ethic is related to how values in general are conceptualized, and is not restricted to euthanasia ethics per se. The euthanasia question, however, may be a major plank in the larger value interpretation. The euthanasia debate may, for some, be primarily the vehicle through which a value interpretation is defended. It may, of course, be just the reverse.

Certain values are absolute and eternal. The worth of human life is one of these. Every human life has some value--there is no such thing as a life not worth living. Thus, under no circumstances should a life be taken. Quality of life is not more important than quantity. Each person's life is sacred and beyond the realm of legitimate interference by another. All lives are of equal worth. (Maguire 1974, Vernon 1974, Weber 1973.)

Wedge interpretation. Any "wedge" driven into the absolute value structure is likely to open a floodgate and lead to more and more killing. The behavior of physicians in Hitler's Germany has been shown by research to support this premise. (Alexander 1949)

Weber (1973: 85) argues that killing is a direct attack upon human well being. Intentions and circumstances are important. Killing in war, cold-blood murder and mercy killing are all different, morally speaking, becuase the circumstances are different. Yet, there is always evil in the act of killing--the evil of rendering a perviously alive person dead--and this evil is the starting point for all consider-ations of the morality of any kind of killing.

Societal Considerations

Euthanasia places primary emphasis upon the individual, minimizing the importance of social and societal factors such as the following which one way or another emphasize that no person "is an island." The death of no person is an isolated act.

a. The person doing euthanasia selfishly controls or in-fluences the behavior or the potential behavior of others.

b. How a person dies influences those related to him, with euthanasia typically producing a negative influence.

c. Life is a gift given and protected by the larger community To reject life is to reject the community.

d. Preservation of the group, the community, the society, requires the imposition of limitations upon taking life. In rejecting euthanasia one is protecting his existing and his future community. (Dyck 1973, Lasagna 1970, Niebuhr 1963, Paulson 1973, Tillich 1952)

Recovery Potential

There is always at least a remote chance of recovery. "Miracles do happen." Further, knowledge of medical errors and of other medical practices should make complete, absolute acceptence of any medical diagonsis unacceptable. Established medical ethics specify the preservation of life at all costs. (Kamisar in Downing 1969, Dyck 1973)

Pain

Suffering and the experience of pain may have beneficial consequences.

Discussion

From the Symbolic Interactionist perspective, neither the pro nor the anti   people can utilize any of the empirical characteristics of euthanasia per se or the act or biology of euthanasia to validate their position. Both positions are validated by socially constructed

97

justifications which involve non-referented symbols. It is likely, however, that in social action endeavors each side will attempt to present its position as though it had biological-empirical factors "going for it." Neither will say publically that their position is a socially constructed one. Efforts to change or defend established laws will succeed to the extent that social support can be secured; to the extent that powerful significant opinion makers can be convinced of the validity of a position and thus real-ize it by believing it.

Both sides utilize basically the same components--each however presents a distinctive configuration thereof. Either side can be presented as the religious-moral side. Either can say that they are in support of the dignity of the dying individual. Each selectively draws his boundary lines or his name-lines around a different configuration of meanings. In many cases both continue to use the same label to identify that particular configuration. Each maintains that his is the moral position, without even suggesting that each is a moral position, even though each is different from the other.

Both are defending "life" but life is defined somewhat differently in each case. The whole debate is one part of the societal struggle to decide the meaning of life and death. We are not nearly as sure today as were our ancestors, that we know the meaning of these basic terms.

Each groups works with a different view of the future. One projects us into a future which needs the stabliity of eternal verities to maintain our humanness. The other projects us into a future which is changing so much that we need to construct with our best knowledge and social tools a set of definitions which will facilitate the most adequate adjustment to the changed set of circumstances, or the "stage" upon which our behavior will take place.

Related Research

Euthanasia related research is very limited. We have bits and pieces of evidence but nothing of an in depth nature. What is available is summarized below.

o A mid-1973 Gallup poll revealed that 53% of those interviewed indicated that euthanasia is appropriate "when a person has a disease that cannot be cured." This compares with 36% who approved under the same cricumstances in 1950.

o Drs. Raymond Duff and A. G. M. Campbell studied 299 deaths among 2,171 children treated in the special-care nursery at Yale-New Haven Hospital over a 2 1/2 year period. The group of 256 children who recieved the best treatment modern medicine could provide fared no better than a group of 43 infants who died after parents and doctors jointly decided to withdraw treatment,

o A survey of 250 Chicago internists and surgeons (Maguire 1974) in which 156 responded to a questionnaire, found that 61% favored passive euthanasia, and 72% felt the practice should not be legalized.

o Morison (1973: 60) reports that very few physicians and surgeons do everything possible to prolong life in all cases, especially among the aged. Fewer employ active measures with the avowed purpose of shortening life.

o Maguire (1974) reports that Walter W. Sackett, a Miami general practitioner estimates that three out of four doctors have made similar allowances on one or more occasions. Maguire also indicates that Louis Lasagna points out that decisions on lengthening or shortening life are unavoidable for doctors. "There is no place for the physician to hide."

o Moralist Paul Ramsey of Princeton University (See Maguire 1974: 60) asks "Should cardiac surgery be performed to remove the lesions that are part of the picture in cases of mongolism, from which many mercifully died before the brilliant (medical) developments of recent years?"

o Maguire (1976: 60) further reports that the national press reported on a case at Johns Hopkins University, in which the parents of a mongoloid child who refused to give permission for surgery for their child, found that it took 15 days for the child to succumb, during which the hospital staff had to watch the child struggle for life. Should the parents have taken the child home? Should the courts have intervened? Death may have been a mercy, but the dying process certainly was not.

o Dr. Harmon Smith of Duke University Divinity School has noted that until ten years ago, about 80% of mongoloid babies died and that today 75% survive. (See Maguire 1974: 71)

o Williams (1973: 107) reports on Leo Alexander's 1949 analysis of medical practices and attitudes of German physicians before and during the reign of Nazism in Germany. In it he reports that physicians cooperated in the mass murders. "...started with the acceptance of that attitude, basic in the euthanasia movement, that there is such a thing as life not worthy to be lived. This attitude in the early stages concerned itself merely with the severely and chronically sick. Gradually, the sphere of those to be included in this category was enlarged to include the socially unproductive, the racially unwanted, and finally all non-Germans. But it is important to realize that the infinitely small wedge-in level from which this entire trend of mind received its impetus originated with the attitude toward the nonrehabilitable sick."

o Vernon (1970: 310) asked college age respondents, "Do you approve of mercy killing in cases of extreme suffering?" to which the following responses were secured:

	Number	Per cent
No	784	40.0
Yes	338	17.2
Yes, in some cases	445	22.7
Yes, but only if the lethal agent is self administered or requested by the patient	321	16.4
No Answer	73	3.8

99

o Williams (1973: 90) reports that about 80% of physicians and a similar number of lay persons favored negative euthanasia. Indeed, 80% of the phsyicians polled indicated that they had practiced negative euthanasia.

o A survey by Laws et al. (1971, reported by Williams 1973: 91) conducted among medical students revealed that, if given the opportunity, they felt that they would practice positive euthanasia.

o Blackwell and Talarzyk (1974: 17) in a nationwide survey found the following responses to the question, "What efforts do you believe ought to be made to keep a seriously ill person alive?"

All possible effort including transplants	8.6%
Reasonable efforts for that person's age, physical condition, mental condition and pain	31.4%
After reasonable care has been given, a person ought to be permitted to die a natural death	26.4%
A hopeless patient should not be kept alive by elaborate artificial means	33.6%

o Wenger (1967) reported the results of a survey conducted among 1000 female members of a Good Housekeeping consumer panel. Fifty-three percent agreed that "an incurable sufferer, who is a responsible adult and who wishes to shorten his agony, should be able to ask for death under a procedure which assures all necessary legal safeguards."

Rejection by 71% was received to the statement that every possible medical effort should be made to keep the body alive indefinately, even though the patient is no longer conscious and there is no possibility of recovery. Agreement was provided by 65% that it should be permissible for a doctor to end a dying patient's suffering by discontinuing the medication, such as intravenous feeding which is keeping him alive. Rejection by 72% was indicated for the statement that it should be permissible for a doctor to take an active step to end the life of an incurable patient. A "yes" response was provided by 48% to the statement that if a patient, incurably ill and in great pain, asks to be allowed to die, the doctor should have the power to grant the request.

1. For further discussion see Glenn M. Vernon, Human Interaction: An Introduction to Sociology, 2nd ed. New York: Ronald Press Co., 1972, and Sociology of Death, New York: Ronald Press Co., 1970.

REFERENCES

Academy Reporter, vol. 13, no. 4 April 1968, New York: Academy of Religion and Mental Health.

Alexander, L., 1949. "Medical Science under dictatationship," <u>New England Journal of Medicine</u>. 241: 39-47.

Bard, Bernard and Joseph Fletcher, 1968. "The Right to Die," <u>Atlantic Monthly</u>, 221 (April): 59-64.

Blackwell, Rober D. and W. Wayne Talarzyk. <u>American Attitudes Toward Death and Funerals</u>. Evanston, Ill.: Casket Manufacturers Association of America, Inc.

Douglass, Jack D., 1967. <u>Social Meaning of Suicide</u>, Princeton, N.J.: Princeton University Press.

Downing, A.B., 1969. <u>Euthanasia and the Right to Death</u>. London: Peter Owen.

Dyck, A.J., 1973. "An Alternative to the Ethic of Euthanasia," in Robert H. Williams, ed., <u>To Live and To Die: When, Why and How</u>, New York: Springer-Verlag, pp. 98-112.

Duff, Raymond and A.G.M. Campbell. <u>New England and Journal of Medicine</u>, reported in Time, March 25, 1974, p. 84.

<u>Encyclopedia Americana</u>, New York: Americana Corp. vol. 10, 168: 590-91.

Fletcher, Joseph, 1960. <u>Morals and Medicine</u>. Boston: Beacon Press, see also "The Patient's Right to Die," Harper's Magazine (October): 138-143.

_____1973. "Ethics and Euthanasia," in Robert H. Williams ed., <u>To Live and To Die: When, Why and How</u>, New York: Springer-Verlag, pp. 113-122.

Freeman, Elaine, 1972. "The God Committee," <u>New York Times Magazine</u> (May 21): 84-86.

Gallahue, John, 1963. "Tragedy an Liege," <u>Look</u>, 27 (March 12): 72-74.

Kalish, Richard A., 1965. "The Aged and the Dying Process: The Inevitable Decision." <u>Journal of Social Issues</u>, vol. 21: 87-96.

Kamisar, Y., 1971. "Euthanasia Legislation: Some Non-religious Objections: in A.B. Downing, ed., <u>Euthanasia and the Right to Death</u>. New York: Humanities Press.

Kohl, Marvin. editor, 1975. <u>Beneficient Euthanasia</u>. Buffalo, New York.: Prometheus Books.

Lasagna, L., 1970. "The Prognosis of Death: in O.G. Brim et al., ed., <u>The Dying Patient</u>, New York: Russell Sage Foundation, pp. 80-81.

Laws, E.H., R.J. Bulett, T.R. Boyce, D.J. Thompson and N.K. Brown, 1971. "Views on Euthanasia," <u>J. Med. Ed.</u> 46:540.

Maguire, Daniel C., 1974. "Death by Chance, Death by Choice," <u>Atlantic Monthly</u>, 233 (Jan.): 57-65. See Also "Death, Legal and Illegal" <u>Atlantic Monthly</u> 233 (Feb.): 72-85.

_____1974. Death by Choice. Garden City, N.Y.: Doubleday & Co., Inc.

Merserve, Harry C.m 1975. "Getting out of it," editorial, <u>Journal of Religion and Health</u>, vol. 14: 3-6.

Miller, Lois Mattox, 1960. "Neither Life Nor Death," Reader's Digest 77 (Dec.): 55-59.

Moor, Paul, 1966. Speaking Out: Let the Dying Lie," Saturday Evening Post, vol. 239 (September 10): 12.

Morison, Robert S.m 1973. "Dying," Scientific American, 229 (Sept.): 55-62.

Mutolo, Frances L. - 1974. "The Role of the Nurse in the Care of the Dying Patient," paper prepared for Nursing Symposium, Living, Dying and Those Who Care. Foundation of Thanatology.

Niebuhr, H.R., 1963. The Responsible Self. New York: Harper & Row

Oregon College of Education, 1975. Death and Dying (Proceedings of Three Convocations on the Concept of Death). Monmouth, Oregon; Oregon College of Education Publications.

Paulson, George, 1973. "Who Should Live?" Geriatrics, (March): 132-37.

Ramsey, P. 1970. The Patient as a Person. New Haven: Yale Univ. Press.

Russell, O. Ruth. 1972. "The Right to Choose Death", New York Times, Feb. 14, p. 29.

_____1975. Freedom to Die. New York: Human Sciences Press

Schneidman, Edwin S., 1974. Deaths of Man. Baltimore: Penguin Books, Inc.

Tillich, P., 1952. The Courage to Be. New Haven: Yale Univ. Press.

Vernon, Glenn M., 1970. The Sociology of Death: An Analysis of Death-related Behavior. New York: The Ronald Press Co.

_____1974. "Dying as a Social-Symbolic Process," Humanitas X (Feb.): 21-32.

Weber, Leonard J., 1973. "Against the Control of Death," The American Journal of Nursing (July): 84-85.

Wenger, H. Leslie, 1967. "Should Mercy Killing be Permitted?" Good Housekeeping, 164 (April): 82+

Wilkes, Paul, 1972. "When Do We Have the Right to Die?" Life 72 (Jan. 14): 48-52.

Williams, Robert H.m Ed., To Live and to Die: When, Why and How. New York: Springer-Verlag, and "Propagation, Modification, Termination of Life: Contraception, Abortion, Suicide, Euthanasia," pp. 80-97.

Wilson, Jerry B. 1975. Death by Decision. Philadelphia: The Westminster Press.

CHAPTER 11

GREATER LOVE HATH NO ONE ... *

Glenn M. Vernon
University of Utah

The euthansia analysis presented here utilizes the Socio-symbolic or the Symbolic Interactionist approach to the study of human behavior.[1] This approach is summarized in the ISAS paradigm. "ISAS" represents the statement that the behavior of the Individual is in response to Symbols, is relative to the Audience(s) and relative to the Situation. This incorporates multiple variables and hence a multi-causal perspective or relativity rather than a one-factor determinism. Euthanasia analyses frequently incorporate an oversimplistic interpretation which at times considers the relationship between but two variables when in actuality there are multiple variables involved in very complex ways. Human behavior is very complex.

A basic premise of this approach is that the meaning of euthanasia from which behavior stems is socially constructed and hence always subject to change. It is a human creation. Established meanings change when there seems to be sufficient conflict or dissonance to create widespread societal questions about established "truths" or answers. The U.S. society is in the midst of such a reassessment of some basic death and life facets which in the past seem to have been accepted without question. Concern with euthanasia is related to a concern with abortion, birth control, and many aspect of old age. In a sense these are all part of the same meaning package".

Given the contemporary societal conditions, euthanasia decisions have to be made. We no longer have any choice. This article considers some of the contemporary death meanings which serve to expand understanding of euthanasia-related variables. Hopefully this will lead to decisions which will reflect the many complex societal components which are currently being related to death and life, making such decisions more harmonious with the social conditions in which those affected by such decisions actually live.

Religion and Euthanasia

In their considerations of euthanasia, many introduce religious factors. Religion, in turn, has extensive concerns with death including euthanasia. Religion focuses upon love. Some have in effect deified the loving process and maintained that God is love. Others use an anthropomorphic concept, conceptualizing God as a loving being, maintaining that the only authentic God-human relationship is a loving relationship, indicating that inasmuch as a person has loved the "least of these" he has done it unto God. It is not surprising then that religious concern has been given to considerations of how loving is involved in and related to death, with the related question of what we are in fact doing to others, even the least of these others, when we make certain death-life decisions. There are important euthanasia implications for any such conclusions, some of which will be analyzed here.

*Military Chaplains' Review. Spring 1976 pp. 73-84.

Concerns with God typically get related to high-intensity moral definitions which provide legitimation for important types of behavior. Conversely, high-intensity moral definitions, whatever their origin, typically get related to God definitions. Religious concerns incorporate both components. Our discussion here will involve both.

In our society, we have started to remove long-established taboos about death and as one part of and consequence of, this change to seriously look at many of the previously ignored aspects and implications of euthanasia. It is the purpose of this article to identify and examine some of these.

Moral or Value Hierarchializing

One of the most widely publicized and presumably widely-accepted premises with reference to death and life is the moral premise that preserving biological life is the top over-riding value or the value of highest intensity. This could be restated as a belief that "greater love hath no one than he prolong his life or the life of others to the maximum." There is, it is believed, universal agreement that living is always better than dying. This belief is widely stated and accepted but accumulating research evidence with reference to actual behavior just doesn't support it.[2] As one illustration, it has been found that many older persons report that they fear death much less than they fear living in a dependent incapacitated state.[3] It appears, in fact, that for most of the persons facing death, preserving a positive self image or reputation is of greater importance than preserving one's biological body. A quicker more dignified death is preferable to an undignified prolonged death. For almost everyone, in fact, there appears to be something for which they indicate they would give their life, in order to respect and love themselves. To them the greatest love is giving or shortening their life for the benefit of others. When a forced decision is involved most indicate that they would forfeit their life for the benefit of loved ones, especially family members. The loving relationship is of greater value than the biology of the one person.

It is interesting that many anti-euthanasia defenses are legitimized by Christian teaching, or in the name of Christ. Ignored is the fact that the individual for whom Christianity is named, voluntarily gave his life for what he apparently considered to be a higher value--love of others. There is evidence that in their own realm of living and experiencing, many indicate a willingness to follow this example.

Our understanding of such evaluations is increased if we explore the nature of values per se, to which we now turn attention.

Abstract and Applied Evaluations

Analyses of evaluations, such as those involved in euthanasia, frequently incorporate an unstated and frequently unrecognized assumption that there is just one type of evaluation involved. Utilizing the ISAS orientation, we start with a contrary premise that there are both abstract and applied

104

values and that our understanding of any phenomenon including euthanasia
is expanded if this value distinction is recognized. All human evaluations,
are a very distinctive type of phenomenon. Value definitions involve
concepts of the type called in Symbolic Interactionism language "non-
referented". There is nothing in the empirical world to which these
symbols refer. They do not stand for something else as do other symbols.
They stand alone. Plato called such concepts "pure idea." Shakespeare
recognized this quality when he indicated that beauty (a type of evaluation)
lies in the eyes (symbols) of the beholder. The value does not lie or is
not located in the object evaluated but rather in the evaluations of those
involved. The evaluation is created by the evaluators. It is not an
inherent component of that which is evaluated. This point is emphasized
in the Christian scriptures as follows:

> I know, and am persuaded by the Lord Jesus that there is
> nothing unclean of itself: But to him that esteemeth anything
> to be unclean to him it is unclean. Romans 14:14

> Unto the pure all things are pure: But unto them that are
> defiled and unbelieving is nothing pure, but even their mind
> and conscience is defiled. Titus 1:15

From an ISAS orientation, the evaluative behavior of the individual
is in response to symbols or meaning (value definitions and other definitions)
and is relative to the audience and the situation. The value definitions
are a part of the "symbols" part of the paradigm. Such values are applied
by people (individuals relating to other individuals) in actual experiences.
These are applied values.

When evaluations are considered to be absolute, eternal, unchanging or
irreformable one apparently abstracts the value definition from the larger
ISAS configuration and considers or treats it as though it exists without any qualifiers or "relatives". Being abstracted, it is abstract. It
is not related to any actual human living variables. When viewed in this
way, value definitions have no non-symbolic restrictions or qualifiers.
One is concerned only with meaning systems, not with human behavior.
Theologians, moralists and others may spend time analyzing value systems
to attempt to make the units in the abstract meaning system as harmonious
as possible--in the abstract.

Abstract value definitions, however, take on considerable complexity
when attention moves to the applied level. Ideals or abstractions always
lose something or acquire qualifiers when applied to specific human situations. When applying a given evaluation to a given situation, decisions
have to be made as to which of the multiple variables involved are the most
important variables in a specific episode. These are accordingly given
greatest saliency in a configuration of complex variables. In effect, a
series of abstract evaluations themselves have to be evaluated and a
decision made as to which evaluation in that episode turns out to be the
top priority, over-riding or neutralizing evaluation. The applied evaluation then becomes situation specific rather than universal. Change any
of the paradigm components and the decision about the rank order of high-
intensity value definitions may also change.

Abstract evaluations can be viewed as eternal and absolute. They are eternal if by eternal one means they do not apply to any specific actual situation. Applied evaluations, however, always have a relativistic here-and-now component. In applying evaluations, humans are not robots with behavior completely pre-programmed so that the same value definition can be applied with the same consequences in every situation. Humans rather have the capacity and the necessity of making decisions about their behavior and about their beliefs (meaning or symbols). Humans are "condemned" to decision making. Making intelligent decisions about their behavior and about the meaning of such behavior is certainly one of the most influential and distinctive behaviors in which humans engage.

The complexity of human behavior in general and the necessity for decision making is emphasized by the fact that there is frequently a conflict between what we want and what we want. We want contradictory things. Most decisions are between good and good rather than between good and bad.

We introduce confusion into our thinking about euthanasia if we fail to distinguish applied and abstract evaluations, and treat applied evaluations as though they were abstract. They are not.

Self Preservation and/or Self Destruction

The somewhat trite statement that from the beginning of life an individual is in the process of dying has relevant meaning for our analysis. From the start of life all human experiences have a relationship to or impact upon the dying component of living. It would, in fact, be more accurate to use the label "living-dying experiences" than just "living experiences." Life expectancy is constantly being shortened by many social or living factors. One death-hastening factor is added to another and to another until the totality of death-creating or death-hastening factors outweigh the life-preserving factors. At that time the individual dies biologically. The straw that "breaks the back" or terminates the life is but the last one added to many predeeding ones. No one single straw causes the death or is the singly death-causing factor.

Societal concern, however, has been focused much more extensively upon the terminal period or what we will here call the "euthanasia period" and hence upon the "last" straw than upon the gradually accumulating components (the stack of straws) and has contributed to the conclusion that everything possible should be done to extend the terminal stage as much as possible. Such justification for the terminal extension, however, is frequently presented in a universal rather than applied, time-limited perspective--everyone should always do everything possible to extend all or any life. "Life" is of course something that is involved from conception on, and the terminal life is viewed or interpreted as though it were the same as the preterminal living. The justification statements make no distinction between types of living or living at different periods of the life span. Hence it is concluded that there is no such thing as "life" not worth living.

Such conclusions rest upon the assumption that the decision makers know what life is and conversely what death is and thus when death occurs or when dying takes place. A label incorporating both life and death components might be more accurate and useful for some purposes. The terminal person is dying as well as living and is living as well as dying. Treatment which prolongs life also prolongs dying. A meaningful question with reference to the dying/living ratio is whether there is a point at which the death-dying component should become the major focus of concern. Does the prolonging of life with a preponderance of dying behavior, justify prolonging the dying and delaying the death with its limited life components? Is there a point at which major concern should be with helping a person die with dignity which would typically include dying with a minimum of pain and suffering. If the answer is "yes" then attention should also be given to the fact that there are different types of pain and suffering. Pain related to a damaged self image can be more difficult and intense than pain related to a damaged liver.

Do the living have any obligation to help a person have a good dying experience? Should just any type of dying be equally accepted and encouraged?

Mixing Levels of Analysis

When one starts to study human behavior in general, there are different levels of potential analysis available. This includes (1) the level of interacting persons or the socio-symbolic level, (2) the level of the individual which considers but one person, (3) the biological level or the internal level in which biological entities inside the individual are taken into account. The internalist approach or level can involve increasingly smaller units or levels down to some sub-atomic level. The type of explanations you secure are related to the level at which your analysis is located.

Some accept as a part of their death beliefs the premise that humans have a biologically built-it mechanism such as an "instinct" of some kind for biological self-preservation. They start with awareness that the internal biological mechanisms of humans do not have to be taught to function and adapt to change. The heart, for instance, does not have to be taught to increase its rate of beating when the input of adrenalin increases. The heart responds automatically.

It is then concluded that the individual automatically follows the same behavioral patterns as the heart. The individual (of which the unlearned biological components are a part, but only a part) instinctively or automatically or in an unlearned manner, adapts to changes in a life-preserving, life-extending manner. The thinking is that if the heart automatically adapts in a life-preserving manner, the individual automatically adapts in a life-preserving manner. The major point overlooked is that there is at the individual level a type of behavior which is not found at the sub-individual or internal level. The individual thinks. The heart does not. The heart responds to biological factors. The individual responds to symbol factors. The behavior of the individual is in response to symbols which have socially constructed meaning--not meaning inherently built into them.

Analyses of euthanasia frequently conceptualize the individual as though the behavior of an individual is but a continuation of the behavior of internal biology rather than a distinct type or level phenomena. However, this is not so. A level difference is involved. The distinctiveness of individual level behavior is evident when one observes the manner in which individuals relate to each other. In over-simplified terms, they talk to each other and think about each other. They make decisions about each other. They do not establish biological connections. Even when they come together biologically (as in a hand shake or a sexual embrace) it is the meaning of the biological union which "holds" them together not the biology per se. Individuals can love each other. Hearts or any other sub-individual level entities cannot. Loving requires symbols.

Explanations of death, including euthanasia, which focus attention upon the biology and minimize or ignore the socio-symbolic factors of interacting individuals distort the basic human condition--individuals relating to other human individual utilizing symbols-meaning. Such explanations ignore what might be called the "spiritual" (symbolic) nature of human interaction.

When we consider the applied nature of euthanasia evaluations and couple this with awareness of the nature of socio-symbolic systems which influence the social as well as the biological aspects of humans, it is possible to conclude that humans have an "instinct" for self destruction or for shortening the span of life rather than an "instinct" for self preservation or lengthening the span of life. The "instinct" involved, however, is a societal one rather than a biological one. Such a statement takes into account the life-long process of dying rather than just the "euthanasia period" of dying.

The "euthanasia period" of dying is only one small aspect or portion of the total dying process. As has been suggested, dying is in fact proceeding from the moment of conception. Thousands and thousands of life-shortening experiences are introduced into the living-dying process at many points of the living-dying process. It is impossible for a person to live without having that living influence his dying process. Euthanasia decisions apply to the immediately-prior dying aspects, with the implicit assumption that these are all that should be taken into account. This point will be expanded in a subsequent section of this article.

Death-related behavior is somewhat paradoxical if we fail to take into account the nature of applied values. In actual behavior we don't actually do what our abstract values say we ought to do. We refuse to let those who want to die die, and justify this by invoking abstract universal criteria. Yet, as a society or in the name of society we take the lives or shorten the lives of some who want to live, as in the case of capital punishment, war and in many more not so obvious or somewhat invisible means of shortening life as when we pollute the air, manufacture defective products and engage in violent sports. We "take the lives" or at least permit or force the shortening of the lives of many who want to live longer. It is likely, in fact, that no one ever lives to the maximum possible for his biological make up--or if the biology were somehow permitted to function strictly as a biological phenomenon without any societal or "living" input.

The Roman Catholic Church[4] and others provide a definition of a "just" or a moral war, which turns out to be a definition of just or moral killing. Lives cut short by a "just" war death are thereby given moral justification. Catholics are also told by their church that there are dying conditions in which those in charge are not morally obligated to make heroic or extraordinary efforts to prolong life or delay death. To institute extraordinary efforts in some cases would then be defined as immoral.

Such a moral stance illustrates the previously made point that abstract "thou shalt not kill" statements when applied to specific interaction become applied and in the process acquire qualifiers. The parents of Karen Quinlin for instance, were told according to popular press reports, by their church that to terminate the treatment would be moral.

The concept of "just wars" involves an ISAS perspective. Some types of dying are moral. Others are not. Those who insist upon utilizing only an abstract or "eternal" evaluation system then are faced with somehow justifying deaths which are defined as moral but which violate the eternal-abstract standards. This may be difficult.

Playing God

"Playing God" is one of the phrases to which anyone who seriously investigates the euthanasia conflict is exposed over and over again. Just what "playing God" means, however, is usually not specified with clarity. It is for many an action-oriented concept designed to influence anti-euthanasia behavior rather than an analytic concept. The implicit unstated assumptions of the "playing God" concept need to be explored. Our comprehension of the complexity of the euthanasia conflict will be expanded if we look more closely at some of these unstated assumptions.

It appears that "playing God" means interfering with the human biological processes, especially not letting biological processes run their course in their own unimpeded way. A person then should die when his biology stops or when his biology is ready to die. Dying is a biological process. With reference to euthanasia "playing God": means not letting the death be a biological phenomenon or not letting biological factors "cause" the death.

If "playing God" means influencing human biology, then behaving in such and such a way is discouraged if such interference shortens or influences the very last stages of living. However, "playing God" or influencing biology is encouraged if this means lengthening the time of living especially during the pre-euthanasia period. Such lengthening involves such acts as having an operation, innoculation, diet, disease treatment, etc.

Another paradox is involved. Those who are engaged in doing all they can to supplement biological processes and thus delay a death which would happen very quickly if they stopped "interferring" with the biological processes are frequently the very ones who charge that "interferring with biology" is playing God and hence is an activity better left to God than usurped by humans. Those "playing God" to delay death, ridicule and condemn those who would "play God" to facilitate death.

It is somewhat surprising that those frequently engaged in extensive efforts to delay the death through use of human skills, knowledge and machines conclude that to decide to use such mechanisms is not "playing God". It is just being human. However, to decide to turn off the machines or not to use them in the first place, is "playing God". One set of human decisions is seen as involving humans doing what ought to be left to God to do while the other decisions are seen as doing what ought to be left to humans to do. Each type of decisions influences the biology of humans and either course requires human decisions.

If rather than defining one type of decision as a God-like decision and the other as a human-like decision we consider each to be human decisions we reach different decisions about the death and life aspects of such behavior.

Those who make these "playing God" charges never seem to specify just what it is about the one human decision which justifies "deifying it" or dehumanizing it, and what it is about the other contrary human decision which justifies "humanizing" it. How can one human decision be God's good decision and the other human decision be the "devil's evil" decision? Either influences the biological process of the dying person.

"Playing God" objections tend to ignore the social-symbolic aspects of most deaths, incorporated in the total living experience of individuals. A biological factor or system in fact, literally cannot "do its own thing" or function alone or independent of socio-symbolic factors. No biological system exists in isolation.

"Playing God" interpretations tend to avoid the human responsibility for the timing of death, thru what we might call "supernatural scapegoating."

Further we tend to interpret the "will of God" as functioning within a clock-time rather than an event-time system, or within what we might call a celestial time system designed for eternal living. God decides according to some clock-time or mechanical time system, the hour and the minute a person should die. In an event-time system, the person dies when he is ready to die, not according to some pre-programmed schedule.[5]

The "God" component of the "playing God" concept suggests that the euthanasia objection involved is an objection to humans doing something which interfers with God's will. This then relates to the point to which we now turn attention about how humans reach decisions about the will of God.

Determining the "Will of God"

Some maintain, implicitly if not explicitly, that the will of God is made known through the biology of humans or more precisely through the biological changes. Biological change is caused by God. God "speaks" to humans by doing something to the human body. When the biology changes it is God who is responsible for those changes. This type of thinking is frequently included in evaluations of both birth and death, especially in arguments about birth control and death control.

This thinking seems to ignore the fact that the biological individual always lives in a socio-symbolic environment and in an empirical-natural environment. It endorses by default the premise that NO influence upon when a person dies biologically is exerted by the individual's social experiences, as well as the individual's symbolic-meaning experiences (his decisions) or the meaning he real-izes AND the non-human environment in which he lives and from which he derives his physical-biological sustenance. It fails to take into account the fact that death rates vary from society to society and from one sub-societal group to another.

It is possible to amend the "God speaks thru changing biology" to include the premise that the social-symbolic and the non-human physical environment influences the biological changes but that these change-influencing factors are controlled by God or possibly pre-destined by God. God's will then is involved in or made known through the physical environment, which influences the biological changes, which then are a manifestation of the will of God. All of the factors which contribute to an actual death are then conceptualized as being God controlled. All human living experiences then are controlled by God. Such an interpretation is diametrically opposed to an ISAS perspective. Such interpretations take the "human" component out of human experiences.

The selectivity of the perception in such interpretations is somewhat amazing when one examines it closely. Individuals spend a life time relating to others, being influenced while influencing others, learning meaning or acquiring knowledge from others and dispensing knowledge to others. Individuals spend their life time securing food from the physical environment and at least since the time of Malthus[6] developing a concern with the relationship between food supply and the human living condition, maybe accepting some version of the Eden story that humans in fact live by the sweat of their brow (and die if they do not work hard enough) and then in interpretations of dying they imply that such factors really have no influence upon dying behavior. God speaks or influences thru the biology, but not the society or the environment. Such thinking by ignoring the influence of socio-symbolic factors by default deifies the society-environmental factors which influence the death related biological changes. Such thinking tends to deify the status quo. If God is responsible, why should humans attempt to change the society. On the other hand if humans are seen as being responsible, then an effort on the part of humans to introduce change is appropriate.

Such thinking is facilitated by defining dying as that which happens just prior to death. Such thinking becomes untenable if dying is interpreted as that which goes on all the time.

The human ability to make decisions, especially value-moral decisions is a most distinctive and some would say the most God-like human ability. The Eden story suggests that it was in learning how to consume or use knowledge of good and evil that humans became as the Gods. Such an orientation discredits beliefs that God's will is known thru biological change,

111

suggesting instead that the will of God is known thru the mind of man or thru the decisions which humans make. God's will is known thru the intellectual decisions of humans not thru biology. Actually even the decision that God's will is known biologically is itself a symbolic non-biological phenomenon. Mormons have an expression that the "Glory of God is intelligence" which can be interpreted as also meaning that the glory (or the most God-like quality) of humans is intelligence. This then raises the interesting question of why God would influence the biological changes of humans to express his will but not the more God-like intellectual processes. If God's will is made known thru the intellect of humans, the sincere decision to influence a death then is granted religious-moral legitimation and it is possible to conclude that for specific individuals in specific situations that greater love hath no one that he shorten his life.

From an ISAS perspective then, the most meaningful question about euthanasia is not whether one is for or against euthanasia in some absolute, abstract manner. It is more meaningful to inquiry whether particular types of dying are appropriate for certain types of persons with certain biological conditions, when such dying has certain types of meaning to the person dying as well as to the others to whom his behavior is related in particular situations. Dying behavior is in response to meaning, relative to the audience involved including the self audience and to the situation.

FOOTNOTES

1. For a more detailed discussion of this approach and the ISAS paradigm see Glenn M. Vernon, Human Interaction, 2nd ed., New York: Ronald Press, 1972.

2. See Glenn M. Vernon and William D. Payne. "Myth-Conceptions about Death," Journal of Religion and Health, Vol. 2, January 1973 pp. 63-76.

3. See Glenn M. Vernon, Sociology of Death, New York: Ronald Press, 1970, Chapter 7.

4. See Glenn M. Vernon, Sociology of Religion, New York: McGraw-Hill Book Co. 1962, pp. 141-2.

5. See Glenn M. Vernon, "Dying as a Social-Symbolic Process," Humanitas, Vol. X February 1974, pp. 21-32.

CHAPTER 12

SICK ROLE AND BEREAVEMENT ROLE;
TOWARD A THEORETICAL SYNTHESIS
OF TWO IDEAL TYPES.

By J. D. Robson

INTRODUCTION

Man's day-to-day interaction patterns are effected by a constellation of expectations called roles. These modes of behavior, or patterns of interaction, are generalized abstractions of situation specific responses, legitimized and supported by other actors within a given social (or societal) space.

In order to meaningfully deal with this concept (role) it is imperative to adopt a specific orientation and to explicate a theoretical framework. For the purpose of our analysis we can begin by focusing on the general definitions given by Popitz and Banton. Popitz defines social role as "...an analytical means of comprehending the coherence of social actions, and at the same time a means of construction for the representation of social structures." Banton suggests that we define role as "...a set of norms and expectations applied to the incumbent of a particular position." He further suggests that this allows us to have two distinct approaches to the study of roles: (1) psychological and (2) structural. A psychological approach is likely to concentrate upon how potential roles or role sets are learned and enacted by individuals. The structural orientation is to trace the ways that sharing of norms and expectations creates networks of rights and obligations for various members of society (or societies). We will emphasize the structural approach due to our conceptualization of man's behavior as being socially constructed and situation specific.

Our orientation here is congruent with that of Vernon (1972). That is, that in a given situation an actor will, in relation to an audience and symbols, sort the response patterns available in order to select the pattern that appears to be the most appropriate.

Throughout most of our life situations this process of role selection is well specified and almost standardized; in stressful situations, however, this may not be the case. Due to the uniqueness of the situation these role-responses, may originate as deviance in relationship to both the individual and group normative structures. It is in these situations that man's behavior patterns often emerge through trial and error, and therefore are dependent upon feedback from the audience for legitimation and/or sanctioning.

The purpose of this work is to expand theoretical role analysis to include the concept of specialized roles for special or stressful situations. We intend to synthesize the theoretical unit of the sick role with the component of the bereavement role in terms of their unique behavioral manifestations.

THEORETICAL FRAMEWORK

In order to further handle the unit of role with some uniformity, it now seems necessary to specify it in some depth. The concept of role has been developed in depth in the work of Linton; Parsons; Merton; Biddle and Thomas; Jackson; and others (Gordon 1966; Banton 1965; Hage and Marwell 1968; Marwell and Hage 1970). However, since it has been so widely used and has been defined in so many various ways, our emphasis will be on the more recent work of Popitz (1972).

Popitz (1972:23) formulates the concept of role into a useful analytical framework, beginning with a definition of a social role as "...a cluster of behaviour norms which a certain category of members of a society, or else of a group, has, in contradistinction to others, to fulfill." This definition makes it possible to further delimit the concept through the development of a framework that increases the preciseness of the element behavior norm and more especially, of the role-norm. He says:

> 1.) We term as behaviour norms modes of behaviour which, in a certain situation, are repeated uniformly by all, or by a certain category, of the members of a society or group, and which, in the case of deviation, are asserted by means of negative sanctions against persons deviating.
> 2.) The development of behaviour-norms presupposes that behavioural regularities can be observed ... Situational characteristics must constantly be included as initial conditions which mostly or frequently lead to certain behaviour-sequences. The inclusion of the situation and the processes of abstraction out of which 'like situation' and 'like-behaviour-sequences' result are, as has already been shown, effects of the process of societation itself.
> 3.) We distinguish behaviour-norms from other social regularities by a rather palpable characteristic, e.g. negative sanctions in reaction to deviation behaviour.
> 4.) The concept of role should characterize the special normative situation of the occupants of certain positions.

This framework allows, for the onset of a unique situation (e.g. illness or death), in which the actor's standard roles are inappropriate due to the introduction of a unit of stress (or a stressful situation). At this time, if the behavior patterns, although 'non-normative' and emergent, are accepted, we have the formation of 'legitimized deviance'.[1] This view seems consistent with that of Haber and Smith (1971) who suggest that exceptional behavior must go through the process of normative redefinition and legitimation in order to be accepted as nondeviant. They point out that in some circumstances we develop "new rules of interaction or constitutive norms" allowing us to re-define specific behavior patterns (roles) which might otherwise be considered deviant. Additionally, the process of redefinition and subsequent legitimation allows us to extend these constitutive rules to encourage others to act in a like manner when confronted with a similar situation. For subsequent instances of similar behavior to be considered nondeviant however, they must occur within these newly defined and accepted boundaries. They position parallels that of Cohen(1966:14-15) in which he suggests that a bona fide sick person "is not deviant by virtue of being sick; however, he is now capable of being deviant in ways that only a sick person can be deviant." This tends to support the contention that an individual's role responses are interpreted, classified and defined in terms of situational definitions, and that there may arise situations for which 'special' behaviors are the rule rather than the exception.

---

1 Legitimized deviance is a contrived classification intended to be useful in the description of the change of the status of a role from the position of deviance (or deviant) into a normative context.

In the event of 'non-normal' (special) situations such as the onset of illness and/or bereavement what would otherwise be considered deviant role responses now become role expectations and the prior normalized behaviors assume the label of deviant within the informal parameters of time.

It seems only logical to now initiate a discussion of the role expectancies associated with illness and bereavement, keeping in mind that the models presented are ideal types and, as such, refer only to those structural uniformities that would exist in an ideal situation.

SICK ROLE

The sociological investigation into illness behavior has been a multi-faceted endeavor with widespread disagreement as to the meaning or usefulness of any one approach. For our purposes the delineation of rights and duties presented by Parsons (1951) is the most useable because, as pointed out by Mechanic (1968:173):

> The concept of the 'sick role' is an ideal type in the sense that it is a theoretical model that attempts to depict the patient's behavioral orientations when he seeks medical care, but is not itself a description of empirical reality. It thus constitutes a perspective for viewing patient behavior, although it does not necessarily describe accurately what the patient's behavior will be.

Parsons posits that social behavior occurs in patterns of predictable regularities and that we have institutionalized some of the recurrent responses regardless of their initial relationship to the normative structure. Thus, there has been much support for the contention that an individual in an unintended stressful situation will still select his behavior patterns in relationship to some definitional criteria. It must be pointed out however, that there are many variables affecting behavioral expectations in any situation and subsequently there is much variation in sick role enactment. Even actors with similar cultural backgrounds and symptoms will act differently due to the operation of selective perception. (See Berkanovic, 1972; Kassebaum and Baumann, 1965; Segall, 1976; Thurlow, 1971.)

In keeping with this orientation Parsons (1951:426-437) suggests that the sick role is composed of two rights and two obligations, relative both to the nature and security of the illness.[2] These role components are:

1) ...exemption from normal social role responsibilities, which of course is relative to the nature and severity of the illness.
2) ...the institutionalized expectation that the sick person cannot be expected by 'pulling himself together' to get well by an act of decision or will ... he is in a condition that must 'be taken care of'
3) ...the definition of the state of being ill as itself undesirable with its obligation to want to get well.
4) ...the obligation - in proportion to the severity of the condition, of course - to seek technically competent help...and cooperate with him in the process of trying to get well.

---

2   see also, Kassebaum and Baumann, 1965; Mumford and Skipper 1967; Mechanic, 1962; Mechanic and Volkhart 1961; Petroni 1969, 1971; and Kasl and Cobb, 1966.

BEREAVEMENT ROLE

In co.~narison we find that role behavior in relationship to the death of
a significant other is quite similar to illness behavior patterns. It also
is a form of 'legitimized deviance' that is a 'normal' response to a stressful
situation. As characterized by Parkes (1972:4), "Grief, after all, is a normal
response to a stress which, while rare in the life of each of us, will be
experienced by most sooner or later; and is not commonly thought of as a
mental illness."

In keeping with Parsons' sick role model, then, we can abstract the
following bereavement role components:

1) Exemption from normal responsibilities - relative to the
primariness of the association with the deceased individual.

2) The expectation that the individual cannot be expected to 'get
over it' on his own, therefore, passivity and an emphasis on family
cohesiveness and interaction.

3) The definition of the state of grief as itself undesirable,
with an obligation to want to re-establish an active, or meaningful,
social life.

4) The obligation to seek help, from the family, relevant others,
or some technically competent specialist, depending on the degree
of dissociation.

DISCUSSION

This conception of these roles, then is congruent with our model of factors
affecting stress related role selection. As presented by King (1952:210):

The generalized features of the sick role are thus determinants
of perception in situations of illness. When sickness occurs, the
patient adopts a new set of perceptual expectations relative to his
own behavior, his obligations toward others, and the kind of behavior they owe him.

A position that is also held by Volkart and Michael (1965) in their discussion
of the bereavement role. They conclude that role variations for bereaved
persons are dependent on their differential definitions of the situation
developed in accordance with the "expectations, demands and pressures from
others."

The similarity of these two role obligations is seen by Parkes (1972) who
summarizes this relationship in the suggestion that:

A newly bereaved person is often treated by society in much the
same way as a sick person. Employers expect him to miss work, he
stays at home, and relatives visit and talk in hushed tones. For
a time others take over the responsibility for making decisions
and acting on his behalf.

Since these descriptions of the roles imply a similarity, let us now
compare them on a point-by point basis.

1) _Exemption_. In both circumstances, normal role duties are
exempted and the individuals are expected to allow others to 'act
on their behalf'. For the sick individual this means exclusion
from social responsibility in order to place all of his energy
towards the elimination of the 'unwanted' illness; for the bereaved, this is a time for personal reflection, uninterrupted by
the complications of normal role responsibilities.

2) _Expectation_. Although the component seems to receive more emphasis within the framework of the sick role, it is also present in bereavement behavior. In fact, after the death of a significant other, we often find that friends (relevant others) 'take care of' the family by running errands and generally relieving them of their role responsibilities; often even to the extent of sending in their meals.

3) _Definition and obligation phase_. In this phase, we find that both states are defined as undesirable, and carry strong sanctioning by others to re-enter active social life. In this respect, they are temporary roles and should be relinquished as soon as is realistically possible. A time definition is problematic in this phase due to various patterns of 'time delay', related to such things a severity and type of illness, closeness (both social and geographic) to the deceased, cultural and religious beliefs and self definitions. Examples here range from varying definitions 'cold severity' with their associated behavioral manifestations on the one hand to chronic and/or debilitating illness on the other. While in the case of death one might compare the Orthodox Jewish bereavement role, which has multiple phases extending over an 11 month period, to the modern Christian orientation for a speedy re-entry into active life.

4) _Obligation to seek help phase_. In either situation this phase varies within a subcultural framework. The major differences revolve around the conception of what is considered 'technically competent' help. Since this definition is situationally oriented and socially constructed in relationship to the severity of the illness or grief, help can range from the selection of someone for 'tacit assistance' to the seeking of a technically qualified specialist.

CONCLUSIONS

We may conclude, then, that although roles are somewhat individualistic in nature they are also in response to the symbols, the audience, and the situation. Thus, significant others, or members of the individual's role-set make an important contribution in the determination of this light appear to be certain abstract components that suggest the existence of patterned role regularities. These roles are somewhat standardized for all role players in a given society or social group in reference to legitimate and illegitimate behavior in recurring stressful situations.

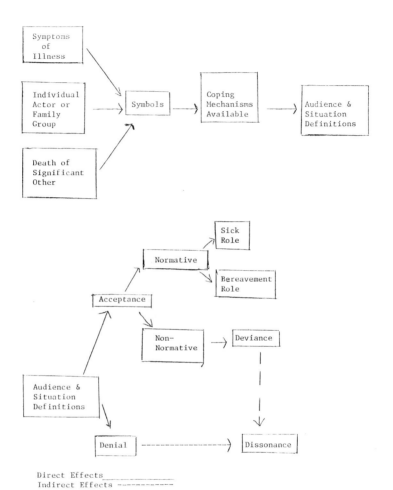

Direct Effects _____
Indirect Effects ------------

Insert 1: Model of relational characteristics of stress-role behavior

REFERENCES

Banton, M.
    1965   Roles: An Introduction to the Study of Social Relations.
            London: Tavistock.

Berkanovic, Emil
    1972   "Lay Conceptions of the Sick Role." Social Forces.
            51 (Sept): 53-64.

Biddle, Bruce J. and Edwin J. Thomas (eds.)
    1966   Role Theory: Concepts and Research. New York:
            John Wiley and Sons.

Cohen, Albert K.
    1966   Deviance and Control. Englewood Cliffs, N. J.:
            Prentice - Hall.

Gordon, Gerald
    1966   Role Theory and Illness. New Haven: College and
            University Press.

Haber, Lawrence D., and Richard T. Smith
    1971   "Disability and deviance: normative adaptations of
            role behavior." American Sociological Review
            36 (February): 87-97.

Hage, Jerald, and Gerald Marwell
    1968   "Toward the development of an empirically based theory
            of role-relationships." Sociometry 31 (June): 200-212.

Jackson, J. A.
    1972   Role. London: Cambridge University Press.

Kasl, Stanislav V., and Sidney Cobb
    1966   "Health, illness behavior and sick role behavior."
            Archives of Environmental Health 12 (February): 246-266.

Kassebaum, G. G., and B. C. Baumann
    1965   "Dimensions of the sick role in chronic illness."
            Journal of Health and Human Behavior 6 (Spring): 16-27.

King, Stanley H.
    1962   Perceptions of Illness and Medical Practice. New York:
            Russell Sage Foundation.

Kutscher, Austin H., and Lillian G. Kutscher (eds.)
    1971   For the Bereaved. New York: Frederick Fell, Inc.

Linton, R.
    1936   The Study of Man. New York: Appleton-Century.

Marwell, Gerald, and Jerald Hage
    1970   "The organization of role-relationships: a systematic
            description." American Sociological Review 35 (October):
            884-900.

Mechanic, David
   1962   "The concept of Illness behavior." Journal of Chronic
           Disease 15: 189-194.

   1968   Medical Sociology: A Selective View. New York: The
           Free Press.

Mechanic, David, and E. H. Volkart
   1961   "Stress, illness behavior and the sick role."
           American Sociological Review 26 (February): 51-58.

Merton, Robert
   1968   Social Theory and Social Structure: enlarged ed.
           Glencoe, Illinois: The Free Press.

Mumford, Emily and J. K. Skipper, Jr.
   1967   Sociology in Hospital Care., New York: Harper and Row.

Parkes, Colin Murray
   1972   Bereavement: Studies of Grief in Adult Life. New York:
           International Universities Press.

Parsons, Talcott
   1951   The Social System. Glencoe, Illinois: The Free Press.

Petroni, Frank A.
   1969   "Significant others and illness behavior: a much
           neglected sick role contingency." The Sociological
           Quarterly 10 (Winter): 32-41.

   1971   "Preferred right to the sick role and illness behavior."
           Social Science and Medicine 5: 645-653.

Popitz, Heinrich
   1972   "The concept of social role as an element of sociological
           theory." Pp. 11-39 in J. A. Jackson (ed.), Role.
           London: Cambridge University Press.

Segall, Alexander
   1976   "The sick role concept: understanding illness behavior."
           Journal of Health and Social Behavior 17 (June): 163-170.

Thurlow, H. J.
   1971   "Illness in relation to life situation and sick role
           tendency." Journal of Psychosomatic Research 15: 73-88.

Vernon, Glenn M.
   1972   Human Interaction. New York: Ronald Press.

Volkart, Edmund H., and Stanley T. Michael
   1965   "Bereavement and mental health." Pp. 272-293 in Robert
           Fulton (ed.), Death and Identity. New York: John Wiley
           and Sons.

CHAPTER 13

SOCIAL EXCHANGE: PROVIDING AN UNDERSTANDING
OF RELIGION AND ITS FUNCTIONS

Michael R. Leming
St. Olaf College

There have been many attempts to discern the functions of religion for society. Discussion in this area, relative to the relationship between religion and death anxiety, has been strongly influenced by the theoretical writings of Malinowski, Radcliffe-Brown, and Homans.

Stated briefly, Bronislaw Malinowski held that religion functioned to relieve the anxiety caused by the crisis experiences which every man encounters in his lifetime. Religion has its origin in the crisis experience because it provides individuals with a means of dealing with extraordinary phenomena. Religion functions to bring about a restoration of normalcy for the individual.

Malinowski (1965) says:

> Every important crisis of human life implies a strong emotional upheaval, mental conflict and possible disintegration. Religion in its ethics sanctifies human life and conduct and becomes perhaps the most powerful force of social control. In its dogmatics it supplies man with strong cohesive forces.

In elaborating on his theory that religion is the "great anxiety reliever," Malinowski turns his attention to the phenomena of death. Malinowski (1965:71) claims that "death, which of all human events is the most upsetting and disorganizing to man's calculations, is perhaps the main source of religious belief." From Malinowski's perspective, death is not only the greatest source of anxiety for man, it is the primary crisis event which calls forth religious behavior. Such theorizing leads us to ask the empirical question, "Does religion provide man with a solace in his attempt to cope with his own death?"

A.R. Radcliffe-Brown, also in the functionalist tradition, disagrees with Malinowski's contention that religion is the great anxiety reliever, and claims that if it were not for religion, man would not have anxiety concerning death. Not concerning himself with the origin of religion, Radcliffe-Brown hypothesizes that religion gives man fears and anxieties from which he would otherwise be free--the fear of spirits, fear of God, of the devil, or of hell. Radcliffe-Brown (1965:81) goes on to say:

. . . in our fears or anxieties as well as in our
hopes, we are conditioned by the community in
which we live. And it is largely by the sharing
of hopes and fears, by what I have called common
concern in events or eventualities that human
beings are linked together in temporary or permanent
associations.

From Radcliffe-Brown's perspective, we would be lead to expect
that the non-religious individual would have relatively less death
anxiety, and would cope better with his own death.

The conflict between these perspectives has been the subject
of discussion for many sociologists and anthropologists. George Homans
(1965) has attempted to resolve this problem by declaring that both
Malinowski and Radcliffe-Brown are correct in their theorizing about
the relationship between religion and death anxiety. Rather than
pitting Radcliffe-Brown against Malinowski, Homans argues that
Radcliffe-Brown's hypothesis is a supplement to Malinowski's theory.
According to Homans (1965:86), Malinowski is looking at the individual,
Radcliffe-Brown at society. Malinowski is saying that the individual
tends to feel anxiety on certain occasions; Radcliffe-Brown is saying
that society expects the individual to feel anxiety on certain occasions.

Homans' treatise is that when individuals encounter death, the
anxiety they experience is compounded by socially ascribed death
fears. Religion with its emphasis on immortality of the soul and
its belief in a coming judgment, increases the level of death anxiety
for individuals who follow the teachings of the religion. However,
once individuals have fulfilled the religious or magical ceremonies
which are required by religion, they experience a reduction of anxiety.

In this article we will attempt to provide a theoretical test
for Homans' theory of anxiety and ritual by investigating the relationship between religiosity and the fear of death. We will hypothesize
that individuals with either high or low religiosity will demonstrate
less death anxiety than individuals who are moderately religious. We
would, therefore, expect to observe a curvilinear relationship between
the variables of religiosity and the fear of death.

The Exchange Perspective

Religion and death anxiety--the theme of our discussion--must be
put into a larger theoretical framework if we are to clearly understand
the arguments of Malinowski, Radcliffe-Brown, and Homans. Properly
understood, George C. Homans, in his attempt to make Radcliffe-Brown's
argument a supplement to Malinowski's theory, is actually reformulating
the theoretical discussions of both men in such a manner as to explain
the two functional points of view by his own exchange theory.

122

Exchange theory is predicated upon the utilitarian assumption that social behavior is reward seeking behavior. Individuals enter into specific interaction with others because they derive benefits from such interaction. Rewarded behavior will be manifested as long as the behavior continues to be rewarded, contingent upon the individual feeling the need for the reward. Individuals will be able to forego immediate reinforcement and even negative rewards (punishments) only as long as they can perceive eventual benefits forthcoming.

Later in this article we will describe, with greater detail, Homans' exchange theoretical perspective. Until then, this brief description of the principles of exchange theory will provide us with the necessary reference point from which we may understand Homans' attempt to recast the theories of Malinowski and Radcliffe-Brown from an exchange model.

Malinowski (1965) claims that death is extremely upsetting and disorganizing to man's calculations and therefore as a diversion tactic men engage in religious activity. For Malinowski, religion serves a psychological function, in that it provides a solace in the face of anxiety. From the exchange perspective, it is the psychological need of the individual which initiates and sustains the exchange relationship which is involved in religious behavior. Demonstrating this psychological emphasis Malinowski (1965) states:

> To the individual who faces death, the belief
> in immortality and the ritual of extreme unction, or
> last comforts (which in one form or another is almost
> universal), confirm his hope that there is a hereafter,
> that it is perhaps not worse than the present life
> and may be better. Thus, the ritual before death
> confirms the emotional outlook which a dying man has
> come to need in his supreme conflict. After death
> the bereaved are thrown into a chaos of emotion,
> which might become dangerous to each of them
> individually and to the community as a whole were
> it not for the ritual.

Malinowski's concern, as demonstrated from the above statement is with the exchange theory which primarily meets personal rather than societal needs. The framework from which Malinowski directs his analysis is psychological--what does religion do for the individual? While the societal point of view is important, Malinowski assumes that what is good for the individual is good for society. This position views the patterns of social integration as being contingent upon psychological processes.

Max Weber, like Malinowski, was also concerned with the needs of individuals in his explanation of the motivation for religious behavior. Weber gives primary attention to what he calls "the problem of meaning."

By this, he referred to the fact that men need not only emotional adjustment, but also cognitive assurance when facing the problems of suffering ^nd death (O'Dea, 1966:11). Every individual is faced with the fact that there are many events in life over which they do not have control. Often times these uncontrollable events frustrate men in their attempts to achieve their goals. It is at this point that "the problem of meaning" arises. Men ask important questions which demand meaningful answers--"Why should I die? Why should a loved one die, and in unfulfilled youth? Why does illness exist?" O'Dea (1966:6-7) points out that religion provides men with a transcendent experience, which will allow them to make sense of their lives.

> Religion, by its reference to a beyond and
> its beliefs concerning man's relationship to that
> beyond, provides a supraempirical view of a larger
> total reality. In the context of this reality, the
> disappointments and frustrations inflicted on
> mankind by uncertainty and impossibility, and by the
> institutionalized order of human society, may be
> seen as meaningful in some ultimate sense, and this
> makes acceptance of and adjustment to them possible.
> Moreover, by showing the norms and rules of society
> to be part of a larger supraempirical ethical order,
> ordained and sanctified by religious belief and
> practice, religion contributes to their enforcement
> when adherence to them contradicts the wishes or
> interests of those affected. Religion answers the
> problem of meaning. It sanctifies the norms of the
> established social order at what we have called the
> 'breaking points,' by providing a grounding for
> beliefs and orientations of men in a view of reality
> that transcends the empirical here-and-now of daily
> experience. Thus not only is cognitive frustration
> overcome, which is involved in the problem of meaning,
> but the emotional adjustments to frustrations and
> deprivations inherent in human life and human society
> are facilitated.

In conclusion to his argument that religion is not only activated by psychological forces, but functions to relieve the anxiety caused by the inevitable tragedies of the human situation, Malinowski (1965:72) makes this very important statement:

> Religion in its ethics sanctifies human life
> and conduct and becomes perhaps the most powerful
> force of social control. In its dogmatics it supplies
> man with strong cohesive forces. It grows out of
> every culture, because knowledge which gives foresight
> fails to overcome fate; because life-long bonds of
> cooperation and mutual interest create sentiments, and
> sentiments rebel against death and dissolution. The

cultural call for religion is highly derived
and indirect but is finally rooted in the way
in which the primary needs of man are satisfied
in culture.

Homans, within the context of his exchange theory, interprets
Malinowski's theory of religion and death anxiety as the interrelation-
ship of activities, interaction, and sentiments. According to Turner
(1974:22):

Activities refer to 'what men do' in a given
situation; interaction denotes the process in which
one unit of activity stimulates a unit of activity
in another person; and sentiments refer to the
internal psychological state of men engaged in
activities and interaction.

From Homans' perspective, Malinowski is saying the men, through
the process of interaction with other individuals and the external
environment, acquire sentiments of anxiety which "rebel against death
and dissolution." These negative sentiments are successfully dispelled
as the individual engages in religious activities. Malinowski's
concentration on psychological exchange establishes what Homans refers
to as the "internal system." This system is internal because it is not
directly conditioned by the external environment but rather by psychological processes which are characteristic of human interaction. After
elaborating upon Radcliffe-Brown's theory, we shall return to this
discussion.

Turning to the theoretical argument of A. R. Radcliffe-Brown, we
find the following statement which poses an alternative to Malinowski's
reasoning (Radcliffe-Brown, 1965:81):

I think that for certain rites it would be
easy to maintain with equal plausibility an exactly
contrary theory, namely, that if it were not for
the existence of the rite and the beliefs associated
with it the individual would feel no anxiety, and
that the psychological effect of the rite is to
create in him a sense of insecurity or danger.

In this quotation, Radcliffe-Brown argues that religion might
serve to increase anxiety for the individual rather than reduce it
as Malinowski would contend. While attacking Malinowski's argument,
Radcliffe-Brown begins with a microfunctional perspective and then
shifts to the macrofunctional point of view as he emphasizes the primacy
of the social function of religion. In the following statement,
Radcliffe-Brown (1965:81), declares that the function of religion is
to create a sense of anxiety which will maintain the social structure
of the society.

Actually in our fears or anxieties as well as in our hopes we are conditioned (as the phrase goes) by the sharing of hopes and fears, by what I have called common concern in events or eventualities, that human beings are linked together in temporary or permanent associations.

From an exchange perspective, Radcliffe-Brown is elaborating upon what Homans calls the external system. The external system involves the elements of group behavior: sentiment, activity, and interaction. The external system attempts to solve the problem: how shall the group survive in its environment (Homans, 1950)? For Radcliffe-Brown, this is accomplished by providing a common concern among the individuals of a given society—the fear of black magic or of spirits or of God or of any other form of retaliation for not performing the religious ritual correctly. Through this common concern society takes on a certain sense of solidarity.

The motivation or sentiment behind group interaction is the quest for societal cohesiveness. Individuals associate themselves with one another as an inevitable outcome of social interaction. This interaction eventually manifests itself in activities or religious rites with the primary function of meeting individual needs. Yet, these rituals also have secondary effects upon the social structure. If persons do not perform rituals correctly, or if they do not follow ritual obligations, they will experience sanctions from the other members of the community. As this normative system (with regard to religious rites) is practiced, it creates a high degree of anxiety and social solidarity.

Radcliffe-Brown's conceptualization of the function of religion is not unlike that of Durkheim's. For Durkheim:

> . . . religion was the sacralization of the traditions, embodying society's requirements for human behavior, upon which society ultimately rests. Society was greater than the individual; it gave him strength and support, and it was the source of the ideas and values which rendered his life meaningful. It made him a social being. The worship of God was seen by Durkheim as the disguised worship of society, the great entity upon which the individual depended.
>
> From this, of course, follows the functions of religion in society. Religion preserved society, kept it before men in terms of its value for them, elicited their reverence for it. In the rites of the cult the society reaffirmed itself in a symbolic acting-out of its attitudes, which strengthening the commonly held attitudes, strengthened society itself. In Durkheim's works '. . . before all, rites are means by which the social group reaffirms itself periodically.' (O'Dea, 1966: 12)

126

Thus far, we have presented the positions of Malinowski and Radcliffe-Brown alluding to a possible interpretation and elaboration of these theoretical discourses from an exchange perspective. From Homans' point of view Radcliffe-Brown's criticism of Malinowski's reasoning does not pose a great problem, in fact Homans would contend that Radcliffe-Brown's treatise is a supplement to Malinowski's theory of religion and death anxiety.

Homans (1965: 87) points out that Malinowski not only says that ritual dispels anxiety, but that this anxiety remains latent so long as ritual is properly performed. According to Homans, Radcliffe-Brown's theory takes Malinowski a necessary further step. The anxiety over performing ritual correctly is dispelled by a secondary ritual which has the function of purifying and expiating the social group. This point is demonstrated by the following observation of W. L. Warner (cited by Homans, 1965: 87):

> The Murngin in their logic of controlling nature assume that there is a direct connection between social units and different aspects of nature, and that the control of nature lies in the proper control and treatment of social organization. Properly to control the social organization, the rituals must also be held which rid society of its uncleanliness. The society is disciplined by threat of what will happen to nature, the provider, if the members of the group misbehave.

Homans (1965: 87-88) concludes his synthesis of the theories of Malinowski and Radcliffe-Brown by citing seven elements related to the study of religious ritual and anxiety. The seven are the following:

1. <u>Primary anxiety</u>. Whenever a man desires the accomplishment of certain results and does not possess the techniques which will make him successful, he feels a sentiment which we call anxiety.

2. <u>Primary ritual</u>. Under these circumstances, he tends to perform actions which have no practical result and which we call ritual. But he is not simply an individual. He is a member of a society with definite traditions, and among other things society determines the form of the ritual and expects him to perform the ritual on the appropriate occasions.

3. <u>Secondary anxiety</u>. When a man has followed the technical procedures at his command and performed the traditional rituals, his primary anxiety remains latent. We say that the rites give him confidence. Under these circumstances, he will feel anxiety only when the rites themselves are not properly performed. In fact, this attitude becomes generalized, and anxiety is felt whenever any one of the traditions of society is not observed. This anxiety may be called secondary or displaced anxiety.

4. _Secondary ritual_. This is the ritual of purification and expiation which has the function of dispelling secondary anxiety. Its form and performance, like those of primary ritual, may or may not be socially determined.

5. _Rationalization_. This element includes a system of beliefs which are associated with the rituals. They may be very simple: such statements as that the performance of a certain magic does ensure the catching of fish, or that if an Andaman mother and father do not observe the food taboos they will be sick. The statements may be very elaborate. Such are the statements which accompany the fundamental rituals of any society: the equivalents of the Mass of the Catholic Church.

6. _Symbolization_. Since the form of ritual action is not determined by the nature of a practical result to be accomplished, it can be determined by other factors. We say that it is symbolic, and each society has its own vocabulary of symbols. Some of the symbolism is relatively simple; for example, the symbolism of sympathies and antipathies. Some is complicated. In particular, certain of the rituals of a society, and those the most important, make symbolic reference to the fundamental myths of the society. The ceremonies of the Murngin make reference to the fundamental myths of that society just as surely as the Mass makes reference to Christ's sacrifice on Calvary.

7. _Function_. Ritual actions do not produce a practical result on the external world--that is one reason why we call them ritual. But to make this statement is not to say that ritual has no function. Its function is not related to the world external to the society but to the internal constitution of the society. It gives the members of the society confidence; it dispels their anxieties; it disciplines the social organization.

In this seven-step conclusion we can see that Homans has carefully brought together the major points of both Malinowski and Radcliffe-Brown. His basic contention is that when individuals experience anxiety in life crisis events, such as death, ritual will be instrumental in making the sentiment latent. However, the fear of violating ritual obligations will again make anxiety manifest. This new anxiety will call for institutionalized ritual and once individuals have fulfilled these religious magical ceremonies which are required by society they will experience a reduction of anxiety.

Having discussed Homans' explicit theory of anxiety and ritual, we shall now turn to his implicit theory of these phenomena. In elaborating upon an implicit theory we must extrapolate Homans' position from his earlier theoretical treatises found in The Human Group (1950) and Social Behavior: Its Elementary Forms (1961). While any exegesis adds to the substantive writings of the author, it is believed that our elaboration will not distort Homans' exchange theory (in the tradition of psychological behaviorism) which is predicated upon a belief in utilitarian self-interest. Abstracting Skinnerian behaviorism, the basic principle of Homan's theory

is that if individuals have needs they will manifest behaviors which
have in the past satisfied those needs. To this basic theorem Homans
adds the following corollaries: (1) individuals will avoid unpleasant
experiences, but will endure limited amounts of them as the cost in
emitting these behavior satisfies overriding needs; (2) individuals
will continue to produce desired and expected effects; (3) as needs are
satisfied by particular behaviors, individuals are less likely to emit
these behaviors until the needs are again present (Turner, 1974: 233).

Applying this theorem and its corollaries to the study of religion
and anxiety, as described by Homans' explicit theory, we find the
following analysis: if an individual encounters an anxiety-producing
situation such as a death of a significant other, and he has utilized
religious symbolizing in the past to define death and dispel anxiety,
he will engage in religious activity to meet his psychological need in
the present situation. Assuming that his sentiment of anxiety was latent
before this present encounter with death, he may have been inactive in
religious ritual behavior and the return to religious experience may
cause anxiety due to the non-observance of religious obligations. While
anxiety may be increased at this time (as Radcliffe-Brown would suggest)
the individual will continue to perform religious behavior as long as he
perceives it as potential for anxiety reduction. When the requirements
for proper religious observance have been met (as determined by the
individual), death anxiety will again become latent.

Another implicit reason for including Radcliffe-Brown's theory as
a supplement to Malinowski's discussion is the need for a balance between
the internal and external systems of Homans' theory. For Homans, social
behavior occurs within the context of three situations--the environment,
the external system and the internal system.

The environment has three main aspects: physical, technical and
social, all of which are interrelated (Homans, 1950). For our interests,
the environment consists of the physiological component of death (the
corpse), death related artifacts (casket, grave, mortuary, grave marker,
etc.), and the individuals who interact within a given society.

The external system, which is the focus of Radcliffe-Brown's theory,
is closely related to the environment. According to Homans (1950: 90),
the external system exists to solve the problem of group survival in the
environment. The external system is external because it is conditioned
by the environment, and it is a system because in it the fundamental
elements of social behavior--sentiment, activity, and interaction--
are mutually dependent (Homans, 1970). The external religious system,
which attempts to provide a solace for death anxiety, is composed of
institutionalized aspects of religion--ritual behavior, role behavior
and collective religious experience. This external system emerges and
is maintained by acting and reacting to the environment. The environment
(like any other stimulus to which individuals respond) does not have any
inherent meaning. Any meaning which the environment possesses is ascribed
to it by an external system. Religion is dependent upon its ability to

convince its followers to accept a particular world view--or a specific definition of the environment. Peter Berger, in his Sacred Canopy (1969), says that the major function of religion is to create a Cosmos (a meaningfully constructed universe) for man to free him from the anxiety of chaos and anomie. In Berger's (1969: 27-28) words:

> It can be said that religion has played a strategic part in the human enterprise of world-building. Religion implies the farthest reach of man's self-externalization, of his infusion of reality with his own meanings. Religion implies that human order is projected into the totality of being. Put differently, religion is the audacious attempt to conceive of the entire universe as being humanly significant.

Yet, once an external system is called into existence it must be maintained if its survival is to be assured. In our case, religion must continually reaffirm the potential threat of chaos and anomie, which will unite individuals through a "common concern." Homans (1950: 109) makes this point in the following observation:

> When a number of persons have come together to form a group, their behavior never holds to its first pattern. Social life is never wholly utilitarian: it elaborates itself, complicates itself, beyond the demands of the original situation. The elaboration brings changes in the motives of individuals. But the elaboration also means changes in their activities and interactions--changes in fact, in the organization of the group as a whole.

In Social Behavior: Its Elementary Forms, Homans (1961: 381) goes on to apply these principles to death related behavior.

> Once a number of people have cried a number of times at a number of deaths, they begin to make a norm of it-- to say that it is the thing one does or ought to do--and the verbal statement of a rule is the first step in the making of an institution. Then other members of their group, whose eyes would otherwise have been dry, may find themselves crying too, because other rewards and punishments have come to sanction the behavior. If they do not cry, they fail in showing respect for the dead, and so lose the esteem of people who are sincere in weeping. Since they do not feel much themselves, they will be ready to adopt as a convention any idiom of mourning the others offer them. And the first thing you know, the formal expression of grief at a bereavement has become an institution, taught to younger members of the society as part of their manners. No doubt the origin of many institutions is of this sort. The behavior once reinforced for some people in one way, which I call primary, is maintained in a larger number of

people by other sorts of reinforcement, in particular
by such general reinforcers as social approval. Since
the behavior does not come naturally to these others,
they must be told how they are to behave--hence the
verbal description of behavior, the norm.

In summary, Radcliffe-Brown's theoretical contribution of an
external system is a necessary component for Homans' exchange theory of
religion and death anxiety.

The internal system, which is of more interest to Homans, is the
primary theme of Malinowski. For Homans, the internal system operates
within the constraints imposed by the external system and which is composed
on the interrelated elements of activities, interactions and sentiments
of groups members (Turner, 1974: 225). However, these elements do not
take quite the same form they do in the external system. Instead of the
motives for being involved in religious institutions, we are concerned
with the sentiments experienced by individuals involved in religious
activity. Unlike prescribed ritual obligations, we are interested in
private devotional activities. Finally, rather than dealing with interaction which is formal in nature such as the relationships between clergy
and laity, our concern is with gemeinschaft relationships of "fellowship
among the brethren."

The focus of attention for the internal system is individual anxiety
reduction. The internal system deals with the psychological effect of
what Vernon (1972) calls "Individual Religion." This emergent and non-
institutionalized component of religiosity is a significant yet overlooked
phenomenon. Elaborating upon Malinowski and Homans, we might contend that
it is the internal system (called forth by the external system) which is
responsible for the positive function of anxiety reduction. Going one
step further, we could argue that institutionalized religion produces
anxiety, while individual religion makes anxiety latent. Therefore, it
is the internal system with its emphasis upon the individual which is
instrumental in deriving the positive benefits from religion. Consequently,
Homans (as an exchange behavioralist) places Radcliffe-Brown's theory in
a subordinate position to that of Malinowski's which emphasizes psychological
exchange. Yet, Homans is careful to acknowledge the need for and the
contribution of Radcliffe-Brown's supplement.

In conclusion, Homans' exchange theory states that religion functions to
relieve anxiety associated crisis situations. Death Anxiety calls forth
religious activity which serves to make anxiety latent. However, in order
to maintain the external system of religious activity (which eventually
becomes institutionalized), the group must continually reaffirm the
potential threat of anxiety to unite individuals through a "common concern."
This secondary anxiety may be effectively relieved through the group
rituals of purification and expiation. However, primary reduction of
anxiety is operative within the internal system of individual religion.

Criticism and Modification of Homans' Theory

While Homan's theory of religion and death anxiety provides for an elaborate analysis of the dynamics involved in this relationship, his treatise is lacking in two major points.

The first problem is that he does not discuss the origin of what he calls "needs." He seems to assume that all needs are biologically determined and therefore, do not have to be explained. While many needs do have biological motivators, all needs must be socially identified. Culture, not biology, specifies what individuals "need." Americans claim that they need toilet paper, while citizens of India feel no such need. American culture defines anxiety as something which is to be avoided by people. However, it is entirely possible that some individuals might enjoy anxiety concerning death and may not wish to reduce such feelings.

Related to this discussion of "needs," our second criticism is of Homans' assumption that death is something which is to be feared. Death may be experienced as extremely "upsetting and disorganizing" to man's calculations, but it is also possible to view death as just another event in life which makes living exciting. The threat of death for the race car driver, the pilot, the skier, and other thrill seekers may be an important motivation for participating in dangerous activities. Like needs, anxiety is something which is socially defined.

Homans' theory may be strengthened by adding a phenomenological perspective to his exchange model. In adding to this theoretical perspective, we not only add to the explanatory power of our existing theory, but we gain a better insight into the etiology of death anxiety.

Peter Berger (1967) describes the process whereby our culture is socially constructed. In his description of the social construction of reality, he claims that the human is both the creator and the product of society. While this may seem contradictory, Berger says that it reflects the inherently dialectic character of the societal phenomenon. While Berger does not explicitly say that it is our human ancestors who were responsible for socially constructing our society, this is in fact the case. Very few of us, if any, are responsible for modifying culture. Therefore, when Berger refers to men socially constructing society, he is really saying that our human ancestors are involved in the process of creation.

The dialectical process in society, of which Berger speaks, consists of three moments or steps. They are externalization, objectivation, and internalization.

Externalization is the process whereby the symbolic world is socially constructed. Through externalization, men create meaning systems which are consensually ascribed to the "real" world. These meaning systems become the basic component of society, and there can be no social reality apart from men creating it. It is this meaning context of society which provides order in and for society.

132

Objectivation is the process whereby the product of man's creation (e.g., the meaning systems) is given a sense of existence independent of its creator. That is to say, the product of man's creation takes on a reality sui generis. Humans, unlike other animals, do not respond to the world per se, but rather to the symbols (or meanings) which represent the world. Objectivation makes it possible for individuals to respond to a socially constructed meaning system.

Internalization is the process whereby men reappropriate the product of their creation and transform the structure of the external and objective world into the structure of their subjective consciousness. That is to say, they make real or "real-ize" their product. For example, Berger (1967:9) says:

> Man invents a language and then finds that both his speaking and his thinking are dominated by its grammar. Man produces values and discovers that he feels guilt when his contravenes them.

This process of internalization is the causative agent which produces a social being out of a biological one. Therefore, Berger seems justified in concluding that in making society, men socially make themselves.

Turning to the phenomenon of death, we can see that any meaning that death has must be socially constructed in the manner described above. Death is neither inherently fearful nor non-fearful. Therefore, any fear which men experience with regard to death is a consequence of fearful definitions which are socially ascribed to death.

It is interesting to note that people turn to institutions for anxiety reduction even though these institutions are responsible for some of the anxiety they experience. Religion heightens anxiety by teaching that there is a divine judgment, where some will be saved and others damned. Yet, religion may also reduce anxiety by providing the means whereby an individual may be included among the saved. The following statement by Vernon (1970: 197) illustrates the dual consequences of institutionalized religion:

> . . . if the goal of the church is to help an individual overcome his evilness or sinfulness, it must first convince the individual that his behavior is evil or sinful. The necessity for such prior socialization is emphasized by the fact that the evilness or righteousness of anything is not an empirical quality of the thing itself, but is rather an evaluation quality which man makes of the behavior. . . . Apparently what might have happened to individuals who evidence high fears of death is that, from the whole configuration of 'you are evil--you can be religiously saved' teachings to which he was exposed, the 'you are evil' aspect, for some reason, was given the greatest saliency. . . the church goal of teaching

individuals to live in constant anticipation
of death, may have, for those individuals, produced
more fear than was intended by the church. The fear-
producing variables were apparently given greater
priority than the peace-producing variables.

Continuing with Vernon's analysis, religious individuals who evidence low
death fears will have given the teaching "you can be religiously saved"
greater saliency. Through adherence to religious obligations the
individual may become convinced of his righteousness and begin to
anticipate future rewards in the afterlife. Institutionalized religion,
for such an individual, will serve the function of anxiety reduction.

Having supplemented Homans' exchange theory with elements of
the phenomenological perspective we arrive at the following theoretical
model for the relationship between religiosity and death anxiety: individuals
do not respond to death per se but to meanings which have been socially
ascribed to death. These death meanings are learned as part of the
socialization process. Concomitantly, individuals learn that they may
resolve their problems through social cooperation and institutional
participation. Institutional solidarity in religion is fostered by giving
participants a sense of anxiety concerning death and uniting them through
a common concern. If the institution of religion is to remain viable,
it must also provide a means for anxiety reduction. Through its promise
of a reward in the afterlife, and its redefinition of the negative effects
of death on the temporal life of the individual, religion diminishes the
fear which it has ascribed to death and reduces anxiety definitions
attributed to death by secular society.

Consequently, our theoretical model would lead us to expect that
those individuals who are either non-religious (persons who do not share
the "common concern" produced by religion) or very religious (persons
who have satisfied the requirements of religion) would have a tendency
to display lower death anxiety than individuals who are moderately religious.
Furthermore, those individuals who are the most religious (in both the
individual and institutionalized forms of religion) should experience the
least anxiety of all. Therefore, the empirical relationship between the
variables of reliosity and the fear of death should be curvilinear with
the most religious displaying the least amount of death fear. (Table 1
provides a summarizing model for the relationship between religiosity
and death anxiety.)

Empirical Verification

In order to provide an empirical test of our theoretical model of
the relationship between religiosity and death anxiety, data were collected
on 403 subjects who were randomly selected employing a multi-staged cluster
sample of Weber County (Utah) residents. Interview schedules were administered
to the 403 heads of households or spouses of the head of the households.
The instrument consisted of various background items, the Boyar (22 items)
Fear of Death Scale and ten items developed by Glock and Stark (1968), and
Faulkner and DeJong (1966) to assess religiosity.

134

Table 1

A Model for the Relationship Between Religiosity and Death Anxiety

	Death-Related Meanings or Beliefs		Death-Related Behavior or Rituals	
	Individual Focus	Societal Focus	Individual Focus	Societal Focus
Malinowski	Death fears are bio-logically determined. Death is inherently fearful. Malinowski assumes that all men fear death.	While death fears are shared by all members of a society, they are individual in nature.	Death fears are reduced by religion to meet the needs of individuals.	Religion is provided by society in order that death anxiety may be reduced.
Radcliffe-Brown	Death is not inherently fearful, individuals learn to fear death.	Death fears are created by religion in order to meet institutional needs--the perpetuation of the institution and the creation of a sense of cohesiveness.	Individuals experience death anxiety if they do not meet religious obligations or properly perform religious ritual.	Death fears are reduced by religion in socially prescribed ways.

135

Table 1. Continued.

| | Death-Related Meanings or Beliefs | | Death-Related Behavior or Rituals | |
	Individual Focus	Societal Focus	Individual Focus	Societal Focus
Homans	Individuals inherently need to reduce death anxiety.	Death fears are increased by religion because individuals fail to honor religious obligations.	Individuals seek anxiety relief through religious participation. This is exchange behavior because anxiety is temporarily increased.	In reducing death anxiety for individual, religion serves the latent function of adding to social solidarity.
Berger	Fears are not instinctual.	Fears are socially constructed as are all other meanings.		Fears are socially reduced.
Lenting	Individuals do not inherently fear death; they are taught to fear.	Death fears are socially constructed. Consequently, people with high or medium religiosity have high fears and people with no religiosity have low death anxiety.	Individuals will experience death anxiety if they do not meet their religious obligations. If they satisfy these obligations, anxiety will be reduced.	Religion provides high anxiety reduction for the very religious, no anxiety reductions for the non-religious, and increases anxiety for the moderately religious.

136

Correlating our religiosity scale with Boyar's Fear of Death
Scale and controlling for the factors of age, education, and religious
preference; we have noted a curvilinear relationship between religiosity
and death anxiety. We have tested the form of this relationship through
analysis of variance by comparing values of Pearson's r with the values
of Eta and have demonstrated the relationship between religiosity and
fear of death is not linear. From our analysis, it is apparent that
individuals who are either very religious or non-religious have a tendency
to display lower death anxiety than individuals who are moderately religious.
Our findings clearly support our contention that religion arouses a sense
of anxiety concerning death and then alleviates the anxiety it creates.
In the words of another, "Religion serves the dual function of afflicting
the comforted and comforting the afflicted."

References

Berger, Peter
1963   Invitation to Sociology. New York: Doubleday, Anchor.

Boyar, J. I.
1964   "The construction and partial validation of a scale for the measurement of the fear of death." Unpublished Doctoral Dissertation, University of Rochester.

Faulkner, Joseph and Gordon F. DeJong
1966   "Religiosity in 5-D: an empirical analysis." Social Forces 45: 246-54.

Glock, Charles Y.
1962   "On the study of religious commitment." Religious Education (Research Supplement) 42 (July/August): S98-110.

Homans
1950   The Human Group. New York: Harcourt Brace Jovanovich.

1961   Social Behavior: Its Elementary Forms. New York: Harcourt Brace Jovanovich.

1965   "Anxiety and ritual: the theories of Malinowski and Radcliffe-Brown." Pp. 83-88 in William A. Lessa and Evon Z. Vogt (ed.). Reader in Comparative Religion: An Anthropological Approach. New York: Harper and Row.

Malinowski, B.
1965   "The role of magic and religion." Pp. 63-72 in William A. Lessa and Evon Z. Vogt (eds.), Reader in Comparative Religion: An Anthropological Approach. New York: Harper and Row.

O'Dea, Thomas F.
1966   The Sociology of Religion. Englewood Cliffs: Prentice-Hall.

Radcliffe-Brown, A. R.
1965   "Taboo," Pp. 73-82 in William A. Lessa and Evon Z. Vogt (eds.), Reader in Comparative Religion: An Anthropological Approach. New York: Harper and Row.

Turner, Jonathan H.
1974   The Structure of Sociological Theory. Homewood, Ill.: The Dorsey Press.

Vernon, Glenn M.
1972   Types and Dimensions of Religion. Salt Lake City: Association for the Study of Religion.

CHAPTER 14

DEATH AND RELIGION
Some Theoretical Aspects

Glenn M. Vernon

Sociologists of religion have problems defining religion. They, however, have no monopoly upon such problems. Religionists have problems also. Lay persons are not immune. Individuals in each category frequently speak as 'one having authority.' Whether we realize it or not we are somewhat at the mercy of our definitions--being, as humans, both slaves to and masters over our symbols. Some of the problems associated with definitions of religion, including the blinders involved will be given attention here.

We will focus attention first upon definitions relating religion to death and other negative aspects of the human condition. We will then, in effect, reverse our field, and consider definitions which emphasize the positive aspects of living. We will conclude with an analysis of a contemporary symbolic interactionist or a socio-symbolic interpretation which seems capable of incorporating both positive and negative or both death and life components, and which provides greater understanding than either of the other definitions of the actual functions or consequences of religion.

Definitions emphasizing death and other negatives

There are those who conceptualize religion as being the human response to negative aspects of living, with death being frequently identified as the ultimate human negative. Also frequently included in this category are experiences involving insecurity, deprivation and anxieties. Fear of death has been hypothesized by some such as Malinowski (1965) as being of such crucial importance that it was involved in the origin of religion. He theorized that it was from awareness of death that humans created beliefs about God and an afterlife and developed rituals relative thereto. Thus, it was maintained that it is in the confrontation of death that the functions of religion are most apparent.

Yinger (1957) has defined religion as "a system of beliefs and practices by means of which a group of people struggles with these ultimate problems of human life. It expresses their refusal to capitulate to death, to give up in the face of frustration, to allow hostility to tear apart their human associations." He continues that "the quality of being religious, seen from the individual point of view, implies two things: first, a belief that evil, pain, bewilderment, and injustice are fundamental facts of existence; and second, a set of practices and related sanctioned beliefs that express a conviction that man can ultimately be saved from those facts."

In harmony with his orientation, Yinger quotes Niebuhr (1968) as answering the question of why religion has persisted as follows:

> ...But life is full of ills and hazards, of natural and
> historical evils, so that this childlike trust will soon be
> dissipated if maturity cannot devise a method of transmuting

the basic trust of childhood, based on obvious security, to a
faith which transcends the incoherences, incongruities and ills
of life.

Sapir (1951) defines religion as the human effort to transform "omni-
present fear" and "vast humility" into "bedrock security."

O'Dea (1966) indicates that religion meets three fundamental conditions
of human living: (1) Contingency, (2) Powerlessness and (3) scarcity.
Religion then is seen as involving the human response to frustration and
deprivation. Religion is introduced into human interaction at the "breaking
points of life." Religion was created from such experiences.

The conclusion that religion is the opiate or the tranquilizer of the
masses also implies that religion is used (if not created) to meet the
negative aspects of living.

Ultimate Concerns

If religion is defined as being concerned with the ultimate problems
of human life, there is a question of just what it is that leads to the
conclusion that death or some other negative phenomenon should be considered
to be ultimate. Among those who make such statements about "ultimates"
as far as is known, no one seems to have clearly specified how it was
decided that death is in fact the ultimate problem.

How is ultimate measured or decided? With whose ultimates are we
concerned? Do we assume that everyone shares the same beliefs as to what
is ultimate? Are the ultimates of concern tentative or absolute? Are
given ultimates always ultimate? If ultimates are absolute and eternal
how then can we explain changes? Are ultimates ultimate only in the abstract
and thus always become tentative when applied by real live people in interaction with other people in real situations?

Death is frequently categorized as the ultimate concern of humans.
However, since for most persons at least there is something for which they
would accept death or for which they would give their life, it would seem
to be appropriate to ask how it was determined that death concerns are
ultimate concerns. There appears to be something more important, valuable
and of higher saliency than death concerns. These tend to center around
self respect and love of others--significant others.

From the socio-symbolic perspective, it would be concluded on theoretical
grounds that what is defined as ultimate may vary from group to group and
from time to time. Definitions are socially constructed. An ultimate
definition can, however, still be used--religion concerns whatever the group
elevates to ultimate concern--and it is not necessarily death related.
"Ultimate" as a concept is contentless, being a concept which ranks other
content elements. It can, then, vary with social conditions. "Ultimate"
concerns how something is believed rather than what it is that is believed.

It is difficult to accept the premise that death is necessarily the
ultimate concern of all humans.

Love of Living and Religion

Let us now, in effect, reverse our field of analysis and ask about positives the questions which have been asked about negatives and their relation to religion. The thinking leading to these negative definitions of religion seems to assume or to accept without much question that it is the negative aspects of living which are somehow problematic or which call for "supernatural" or extra-ordinary explanations/ interpretations and legitimation/validation. Why? Who do high-intensity negatives and not high-intensity positives call for high-intensity legitimation?

What happens to our definition of religion if we, in fact, focus attention upon the "flipside" or the reverse of those variables typically incorporated in such negative definitions of religion? Is one any more ultimate than the other? Is one potentially any more disruptive of social relationships than the other? For that matter is disruption more problematic or more productive of problems than stability?

Some of the "melodies" or themes from the two sides of our "religion record" can be presented as follows:

Negative	Positive
Death	Life
Frustration	Fulfillment, satisfaction
Hostility	Acceptance, helping
Evil	Good
Pain	Health and feeling well
Bewilderment	Knowing, understanding
Injustice	Justice
Fear	Nonfear, faith, acceptance
Insecurity	Security
Contingency	Certainty
Powerlessness	Powerfulness
Scarcity	Abundance
Deprivation	Plenty

Why have so many accepted without question that it is the negative aspects of life which so demand or call out for answers that humans create and construct their religion on these negative foundations? Why have they accepted the assumption that these characteristics require some type of supernatural or superhuman interpretation or explanation, whereas apparently the reverse or positive side is taken for granted? Are we maybe saying or at least implying that the positive side somehow just goes with being human, whereas the negative does not and thus requires the introduction of some type of superhuman component to explain it? Humans are worthy of their goodness. They don't have to justify it. They do, however, have to justify the evilness found in their society, and in doing this justification they create their religion.

Can't we, however, ask the same questions about negatives? Doesn't frustration and fear go with being human? Isn't death a basic component of living? Humans are "worthy" of their fears, insecurities and other negatives. Such negatives are commensorate with their behavior.

The successes as well as the failures of humans require legitimation and justification. They are potentially just as disruptive of the human social order as are negatives. Success can be as demoralizing as failure. Accomplishing something can produce as much disorganization as the failure to accomplish a goal, unless the success is defined in terms which make it harmonize with the moral standards of the group. One person's success often turns out to be another person's failure. A moral system, if it is to be effective, must take account of both situations.

Economic crisis in one area frequently contributes to economic prosperity in another. One nation wins another loses a war. Unless economic success is defined as being desirable, social sanctions will be brought to bear on those who are economically successful, with the consequent failure of the economic system. An ethical system must provide moral meaning for not only the failures but the successes therein.

It was, then, from the human confrontation with life not death that humans created religion. It was from confronting loving not hating, confidence not fearing, security not insecurity that human constructed religion. From this perspective the human efforts to justify happiness, loving, helping or just being happy and contented lead to the creation of religion.

Such an analysis acquires strength from a realization of the strength of loving. The high intensity nature of such experiences can be interpreted as of such quality that it cannot be adequately explained as just a human achievement or a "natural characteristic." Any experience which produces such highly intense reactions then must involve something superhuman or supernatural. Some type of god concept then was necessary to obtain meaning closure or to adequately explain such experiences. Further, if there were no god, humans would invent one in order to justify their positive experiences.

Some many have unconsciously assumed that only negative experiences have to be explained, defined, labeled and evaluated, rather than that all experiences, however evaluated, have to be named and explained. if they are going to be taken into account.

Socio-Symbolic Perspective

An alternate to both the insecurity-derived religion and the security-derived religion is security-insecurity-derived religion. Such an interpretation is provided by a socio-symbolic perspective. From this perspective, humans, defined as symbol or culture-knowledge using beings whose behavior is in response to the meaning of whatever symbols-culture they real-ize or believe, have been religious from that point (whatever, wherever or whenever it was) where they could transcend the empirical world and respond to symbols or to arbitrarily created meaning which had no empirical referent. Actually there may have been no "point" at which this human symboling ability was created since the development may have been a gradual development rather than a turning-the-corner or "from this point on" sort of experience.

The religious component of behavior or interaction, all of which is in response to meaning or symbols is that involved in the high intensity components of interaction. Those experiences experienced most intently would seem to merit distinctive explanations or "causative factors" to explain why they are different from the more routine, run-of-the-mill, everyday aspects of living.

142

Thus in the pattern of the symbol-responding beings they were, humans tended to suit the answer to the question, or adapt the symbolic causes to the symbolic consequences. High-intensity experiences call for high-intensity causes. Extra-ordinary events are the result of extra-ordinary causes.

The "gods" or the god concepts thus created can be applied equally well to the negative frustration components and to the positive satisfaction components either of which could be of a high intensity nature.

From this orientation, our definitions of religion turns out to include the high-intensity value definitions or the high-intensity legitimation validation definitions and/or definitions of the supernatural related thereto, plus behavior related to these definitions. Both beliefs and behavior are included.

And, again, such beliefs/behavior can be either positive or negative.

What we have done is to combine the other two interpretations or abstracted the common denominator which turns out to be high intensitness. This includes high-intensity moral definitions plus high-intensity audience definitions.

Religion is an expression of the human awareness of the socio-symbolic nature of the human condition. It is an expression of awareness that humans are by their very nature social in behavior and that social behavior by its very nature is symboled in nature. Behavior of interacting individuals is in response to symbols (meaning or definitions).

The socio-symbolic theory permits us to explain both the anxiety-death-fear aspects of religion and the loving-affection-rewarding-satisfying aspects. The consequences of any particular religious component are relative, and being relative may result in love or otherwise, in anxiety or otherwise, depending upon the larger configuration of which that one part is a component.

Value definitions involve non-referented concepts or symbols. These are symbols which facilitate the human use of words, rather than identify some aspect of the empirical non-human world. At the human level, behavior is related to meaning, which is socially constructed. Meaning has to be organized if more than one human is going to respond to it. Word organizing or systematizing symbols then have to be created. If a person is going to combine two parts of hydrogen and one part of oxygen he needs to know more than the two words "hydrogen" and "oxygen." Knowing hydrogen and oxygen does not include knowing anything about what humans should do with H and O. Other words are needed so that action plans or scripts can also be known.

"Transcend the empirical world" is an expression used at times to describe non-referented concepts. Humans with their lack of biological drives have to create "symbol drives" or very strong words, in order to pattern behavior. Use of empirical-earth transcending, or non-referented concepts is a part of religion, or is a spiritual activity.

It is suggestive that in the story of the humanizing of Eve and Adam, it was the learning how to use "knowledge of good and evil" which is non-referented knowledge, which marked the beginning of humanness, and also marked the beginning of being "as the gods", knowing good from evil. Such "knowing" is part of religion.

If one accepts this definitions of religion, he also accepts the premise that everyone is religious. Being religious is a basic component of being human. Differences in the content of religion can be identified and studied but one cannot with just this definitions, study the differences between "religious" and "non-religious" persons. There are no non-religious persons to clasify in that slot. There are only people who are religious in different ways. Those who define their particular religion as being exclusively "religion" or as real religion and thus relegate all those who do not share that religion to a non-religious category are not satisfied with such a definition. Our definition is useful for sociological purposes, but not equally useful for some other purposes.

It has been suggested then that religion developed from, or is the human effort to explain two basic human factors. (1) That humans respond to meaning, which involves symbols which a) re-present but do not duplicate the empirical world and b) which transcend the empirical world, being pure idea or "spiritual: phenomenon. (2) Humans live with, thru and for others, and that most (or many) of the most significant, meaningful, intense experiences involve relating to others.

As a general statement, it is being suggested that religion developed as an identifiable phenomenon, as humans became aware of their basic social and symboled nature--as they became aware that human engage in symboled interaction. Another way of saying this is that religion as it exists in-corporates efforts to explain the socio-symbolic aspects of being human.

Further, the Eden Story suggests that as long as humans have been human they have been religious. The socio-symbolic interpretation harmonizes with such a conclusion.

The Eden Story of the creation identifies the process by which humans became "as the gods." This might be interpreted as the process by which they acquired religion. Some may not agree with that interpretation, however. In any event, the point at which they acquired religion was the event in which they learned how to make their own moral decisions. At the point where they first confronted death, then, they would already be religious or already have a religion. The same thing is true about confronting birth. It would seem in fact, that the ability to make moral decisions preceded both birth and death and further that birth and death were created as a "package deal" in that humans can't have one without the other, and that having the ability to make moral decisions was a prerequisite of both.

Part of the process by which the ability to make moral decisions was acquired involved learning how to say "no" to God and getting away with it. They would, thus, know that the decision was theirs and that they had to live with the consequences thereof. They were responsible. This "no" was the original negative or original sin, although the "sin" concept as usually interpreted does violence to the approach. Being religious is a part of the process of making human decisions. It permeates all of living-- or at least all of the decision-making process. It did not then start from the experience of death or some negative experience or from love-birth or some positive experience. It started from the socially created awareness that a spiritual or symboled world could be created and used in a meaningful manner.

144

The "hidden depths" of human living about which some have written are found to occur or exist in both directions. The components are "hidden" because there is no empirical referent involved with the concepts used. Non-referented concepts acquire their meaning when the humans involved create it. Before it is created, it exists nowhere and thus is indeed "hidden"-- it doesn't exist.

The socio-symbolic interpretation is not as dramatic or spectacular as the "insecurity" or the "security" interpretation. Humans are by their very nature religious. It is just one aspect of being human. From such a perspective, then, one is more easily lead to considerations of both the positive and negative consequences of the content and the practice of any given religion.

Functions of Religion -- statements or questions?

If we start our excursion into the domain of religion with this socio-symbolic definition, we are less likely to conclude that "the function of religion is..." and more likely to ask "Does religion function to achieve such and such goals?" Maybe we will even feed in or introduce greater specificity into our questions and ask, "Does Religion X, or maybe does a certain component or aspect of Religion X, serve to or function to achieve such and such a goal?" Maybe we will introduce even greater specificity into our basic questions by asking variations of the following:

1. Does Religion X (with a known content) serve to achieve such and such a goal, such as reduce the fear of death?

2. Does Religion X function to reduce fear of death equally for particular types of believers such as those who believe in an afterlife and those who do not, or those who believe in God and those who don't?

3. Does Religion X function to reduce fear of death for particular types of believers in particular types of situations, such as in a situation of potential human destruction via nuclear bombs?

From such a perspective we may be more willing to distinguish the death-related functions of types of religion such as societal religion, church religion and the religion of the independents.

Such questions harmonize with available research findings which clearly indicate that religion (in the abstract with no qualifiers) does not have a consistent function or consequence. Religion can reduce fear of death but religion can increase such fears. Religious components of funerals can provide solace and comfort for the bereaved but religious components of funerals can increase anxiety and be disruptive of mental stability. Given the diversity of religions available and the diversity of people involved it is impossible to find any one given religious component which always for all people has the same consequence. Human behavior is much too complex for that.

Summary

It is possible to develop a theory of the creation of religion by using death-related and other high-intensity negative experiences as the "building blocks" from which humans created religion. It is, however, also possible to create a rival interpretation emphasizing the positive-life related high-intensity experiences such as loving, and just as adequately explain the creation and perpetuation of religion.

A socio-symbolic perspective provides an alternate explanation which incorporates the basic components of both the death-related and the life-related theories. A socio-symbolic interpretation suggests that either death or life or theoretically anything else, can be productive of the most intense aspects of living. Whatever the content, the high-intensity components are a basic part of the religion of those who real-ize them.

Death has no monopoly upon such real-izations.

REFERENCES

Malinowski, B. 1965. "The role of magic and religion," pp. 63-72 in William A. Lessa and Evon Z. Vogt, eds., Reader in Comparative Religion: An Anthropological Approach. New York: Harper and Row.

Nieburh, Reinhold, in The Religious Situation: 1968, Donald Cutler, ed. Boston: Beacon Press, p.x.

O'Dea, Thomas F. 1966. The Sociology of Religion, Englewood Cliffs, N.J.: Prentice-Hall, Inc.

Sapir, Edward, in David G. Mandelbaum, ed. Selected Writings of Edward Sapir, in Language, Culture and Personality, University of California Press, Berkeley, 1951, pp. 346-56.

Yinger, Milton J. 1957. Religion, Society and the Individual. New York: The Macmillan Co. and The Scientific Study of Religion, 1970. New York: The Macmillan Co.